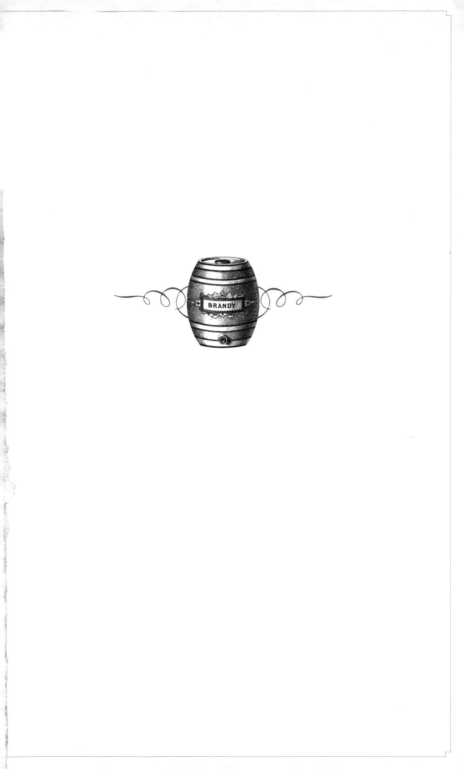

PRAISE FOR LESLEY M. M. BLUME AND *LET'S BRING BACK*

A tongue-in-cheek sparkler of an encyclopedia. Upon reading, you may find yourself in the kitchen, dressed in a silk lap robe and glamour slippers, stirring up a Tipsy Parson that would make Tallulah Bankhead proud.

W MAGAZINE

A humorous ode to preservation and the art of rediscovery. Heartily recommended.

THE WALL STREET JOURNAL

Whimsical ... comical ... delightful ... Blume's book is about more than just populating your life with antique trinkets; it's about curating your own charming lifestyle while celebrating the Wildean ideals of life as art.

THE NEW YORKER

If you're feeling lousy and you read this book, it awakens you to things that have made you happy in your life. It reminds you of a time when certain things, ideas, gestures got you through. [*Let's Bring Back*] promotes and revels in an idea of life that's lived in 3-D, not 2-D, a life lived civicly and civil-y. And that is a very wonderful thing.

SALLY SINGER, Editor, *T: THE NEW YORK TIMES MAGAZINE*

Elegant . . . whimsical . . . As Blume herself might put it, we just think this book is the bee's knees.

O, THE OPRAH MAGAZINE

Wistful . . . zeitgeisty . . . charming . . . *Let's Bring Back* is like a stroll down memory lane. Whether you'd carry a parasol down 5th Avenue or plop it in your caipirinha there's something for everyone.

ELLE

A charming slip of a book ... that quite deliciously and convincingly has the romantics among us pining for the ways of the dearly held past.

CHICAGO TRIBUNE

Library of Congress Cataloging-in-Publication Data is available.

ISBN: 978-1-4521-0826-1

Manufactured in China

DESIGNED BY SUPRIYA KALIDAS

ILLUSTRATIONS BY GRADY MCFERRIN

10 9 8 7 6 5 4 3 2 1

Chronicle Books LLC
680 Second Street
San Francisco, California 94107

WWW.CHRONICLEBOOKS.COM

LET'S·BRING·BACK

THE
❦ COCKTAIL EDITION ❦

A Compendium of

IMPISH, ROMANTIC, AMUSING,

and OCCASIONALLY APPALLING POTATIONS

from BYGONE ERAS

LESLEY M. M. BLUME

Illustrations by Grady McFerrin

CHRONICLE BOOKS
SAN FRANCISCO

TABLE OF CONTENTS

IT IS OFTEN SAID THAT HISTORY EDITS ITSELF FOR A REASON.
The same can be said for the by-products of each epoch's popular culture — and delectables, confections, and libations are no
exception, including the realm of cocktails. As food critic and
historian William Grimes once noted:

> "**M**ixed drinks tend to be invented on a whim,
> named as an afterthought, consumed on the spot
> and forgotten in an instant. Like . . . movies, car-
> toons, television commercials, and funny T-shirts,
> most cocktails earn their oblivion."

Yet even the best editors sometimes make misjudgments,
and history is no exception. Plenty of splendid cocktails have
been rudely shunted aside after falling out of vogue — and
their successors often do not hold a candle to the drinks they
replace.

Introducing *Let's Bring Back: The Cocktail Edition*, a celebra-
tion of once-the-height-of-fashion, now-largely-forgotten
beverages from bygone eras that should be reintroduced
today — or remembered at the very least. The selections in
the following pages—culled from ancient times through the
1960s—are by turns fizzy and flat, sweet and sour, lethal and
prim. Some of them are absurd, others sentimental, and yet
others outright scandalous.

At heart, this book aims to exalt the humor that has always permeated the world of mixology, something strongly reflected in the colorful nomenclature of mixed drinks over the years—and it is in part on this nomenclature that the following drinks have been selected. Among the honorifics assigned to the included cocktails, we find impishness, encounter poignancy, and detect feigned modesty. Thumbing through this tome should feel like meeting a roster of high-spirited, eccentric characters at a party: the Bosom Caresser, for instance, is a charming rake; the Salomé is a sensual, dangerous lady; the Runt's Ambition, you'll find, is quite a little dictator. Holly Golightly could hardly have pulled together a more jovial guest list.

Gravely serious mixologists might bristle at the idea of a compendium of cocktails curated by the merits of their names—but rest assured that most of these old-fangled drinks are actually quite delicious as well (with the exception, perhaps, of the Gingivitis Cocktail, but that concoction has been included for reasons other than its palatability). However, this seems like a good moment to present certain caveats about this book:

Firstly, *Let's Bring Back: The Cocktail Edition* is not meant to be an all-inclusive catalog of history's cocktails; nor is it meant to be an in-depth how-to manual. You will not be instructed on the perfect shaking technique here; nor will you be pestered with a soulful deliberation of the olive versus the twist. Store bookshelves teem with such works, published by some of history's legendary bartenders. Seek these out and you will find a bevy of gifted mentors.

Nor is this book meant to be an earnest history of the evolution of cocktails; again, countless books and Web sites devote themselves to chronicling the origins of classic libations (often without much success, for ascertaining the accurate biographies of cocktails can be a maddening quagmire). Likewise, you should look elsewhere to find recipes for mainstay classic drinks that have already been revived in spades, such as Manhattans, Sidecars, Martinis, and Ward 8's. The drinks celebrated here are more obscure—and yet each brims with personality and eagerly awaits its moment of rediscovery.

But don't worry: This book doesn't leave you in the lurch after making introductions. Each entry also offers its readers guidance about occasions on which to revive each drink. Staring at a long list of forgotten cocktails, how on earth are you supposed to choose one? This is where *Let's Bring Back: The Cocktail Edition* comes in handy. For example, you will be instructed to sip an Algonquin Cocktail when you want to feel witty, revive the Gold Cocktail to celebrate a windfall, and nuzzle a Poor Dear Old Thing Cocktail when you're feeling neglected and woeful (again). Each drink listed in these pages has been assigned that sort of duty, as a way to make itself useful to the modern imbiber.

It's great fun not only to revisit the stories behind the creation of these cocktails, but also to imagine the millions of narratives caused by the drinking of them. The following libations caused faces to be slapped, tears to be shed, babies to be made, fox trots and the Twist to be danced, marriage proposals to be uttered (and perhaps rescinded), and so on. The people who drank these drinks during the heights of their popularity did so for the same reasons we guzzle today's trendy cocktails: to celebrate, to escape, to drown sorrows, to feel bigger, to feel glamorous—or feel nothing at all.

People have drunk for these reasons since the beginning of time, and will continue to do so as long as booze can be squeezed out of grapes and grains. That's one thing that the past will always have in common with the present and the future. The only thing that changes over time is the chariot used to spirit imbibers down intoxication's giddy path.

Without further ado, let's get down to the business of rediscovering some of history's more entertaining concoctions. From the Algonquin to the Zombie, there are many delights to be shaken, stirred, poured, and enjoyed once again.

We stopped and had a drink.

'Certainly like to drink,' Bill said.

'You ought to try it sometime, Jake.'

'You're about a hundred and forty-four ahead of me,' [I said.]

Ernest Hemingway • THE SUN ALSO RISES

BOTTOMS UP

ONE HUNDRED AND FORTY-FOUR DRINKS
TO BE REVIVED & OCCASIONS UPON
WHICH TO REVIVE THEM

ALGONQUIN
Cocktail

❋ TO HELP YOU FEEL WITTY ❋

Drink this vintage concoction to invoke Dorothy Parker and the cruel wits of the famed Algonquin Round Table, of which Parker was the undisputed queen. This delicious viper's nest of writers, critics, and other creative luminaries met daily for an insult-laden luncheon at New York City's Algonquin Hotel, at which wit was the currency. You always had to be on your toes, or you were bled in full view of the others.

Parker herself *never* disappointed. For example, once during a word game, Parker was asked to use the word "horticulture" in a sentence. Without missing a beat, Parker responded: "You can lead a horticulture, but you can't make her think."

"Three and I'm under the table
Four and I'm under the host."

Dorothy Parker • ON THE SUBJECT OF MARTINIS

Mixing together the following ingredients will immediately augment your own wit factor:

1 OUNCE RYE

½ OUNCE FRENCH VERMOUTH

½ OUNCE PINEAPPLE JUICE

ICE CUBES

———

Shake with ice, strain into a chilled cocktail glass, and garnish with a forked tongue.

———

Serves 1

ANGEL'S TIT

Cocktail

❄ TO SHOCK GOODY-GOODIES ❄

People *loved* to scandalize in the 1920s. This outrageous Prohibition favorite is a sensory way to evoke the madcap antics of the time—and scandalize contemporary prisses. Think of it as an impish version of a Shirley Temple.

Those too sanctimonious to suckle an Angel's Tit can seek out the recipes of the more demure Angel's Blush cocktail or an innocent Angel's Wing cocktail.

---

1 OUNCE MARASCHINO LIQUEUR

WHIPPED CREAM

RED CHERRY

Pour liqueur into a chilled pousse-café glass, top with whipped cream, and place a red cherry exactly in the middle.

Serves 1

LET'S BRING BACK: *The Cocktail Edition*

BYGONE BENDERS

HISTORICAL EUPHEMISMS FOR THE WORD "DRUNK"

Over the centuries, thousands of colorful words and phrases have been coined to describe the (sometimes-joyous, often-ignoble) state of inebriation. A sampling thereof:

86'ed	On a jag
Back teeth afloat	On a tear
Banged up to the eyes	On a toot
Bent	Ossified
Blind	Pickeled
Blotto / Blotto'd	Pie-eyed
Can't see a hole in a ladder	Razzle-Dazzled
Dull-eyed	Seeing two moons
Fogged	Sozzled
Full of Dutch courage	Spifflicated
Gone a peg too low	Stewed
Half-seas-over	Stinko
Holding up the lamppost	Three sheets to the wind (number of sheets varies)
In bed with one's boots on	Tight
In drink	Tip merry
In one's cups	Tying one on
In the suds	Zozzled

[PLATE I]

Ants in the Pants

ANTS IN THE PANTS

Cocktail

❊ TO TREAT RESTLESSNESS ❊

The Prohibition era certainly embraced twitching nervousness as a cornerstone of the popular culture: Not only did that epoch give us the wild jitterbug dance, it offered up the now-forgotten Ants in the Pants Cocktail. Examining the ingredient list, however, it appears that the effects were likely curative instead of causal.

---

1 OUNCE GIN

½ OUNCE GRAND MARNIER

½ OUNCE SWEET VERMOUTH

1 DASH FRESH LEMON JUICE

ICE CUBES

1 LEMON PEEL TWIST FOR GARNISH

Shake with ice and strain into a cocktail glass.
Garnish with the lemon peel twist. Administer at first
signs of antsiness, butterflies, or heebie-jeebies.

Serves 1

ARSENIC
&
Old Lace

· Cocktail ·

An old-fashioned concoction named after the iconic 1941 play (and also the 1944 film starring Cary Grant) of the same name. This murder farce featured the antics of two sweet little old ladies who occupy their days baking goodies, hosting the local minister, tending to ill neighbors—and "compassionately" poisoning homeless, family-less old men who happen to shamble into their lace-filled lair.

Have a look at the ingredients below: The gin and absinthe combination provides an excellent "This won't hurt a bit" anesthetic, while the crème de violette adds the perfect dash of old-biddy sweetness.

1½ OUNCES GIN

½ OUNCE ABSINTHE

3 DASHES FRENCH VERMOUTH

3 DASHES CRÈME DE VIOLETTE

ICE CUBES

Shake with ice and strain into a chilled cocktail glass.
Serve to victims with a look of cherubic innocence.

Serves 1

ASTOR

Painless Anesthetic

Cocktail

❄ THE PERFECT PRE-DENTAL VISIT LIBATION ❄

Speaking of anesthetics (see Arsenic and Old Lace Cocktail, opposite), any dentist looking to boost his or her practice should serve up these old cocktails instead of employing the same old boring Novocain. Created originally by the Stork Club for Mary Astor of the venerable Astor clan, this drink packs a wallop and will banish toothaches—and any other sort of aches—in no time at all.

---

3 OUNCES GIN

1 OUNCE FRENCH VERMOUTH

1 OUNCE ITALIAN VERMOUTH

1 OUNCE COGNAC

1 DASH ORANGE BITTERS

ICE CUBES

1 LEMON PEEL TWIST FOR GARNISH

SUGAR FOR SPRINKLING

Shake well with ice cubes, strain into a chilled cocktail glass, garnish with the lemon peel twist and a sprinkling of sugar. Use to rinse your mouth twice daily after brushing your teeth.

Serves 1

PASS THE BUBBLY

Our wise ancestors knew that there really should be an infinite number of ways to enjoy Champagne, and created all sorts of Champagne-related diversions, rituals, and recipes. Some revival-worthy examples:

CHAMPAGNE CROQUET

Croquet used to be wildly popular during the late 1800s, when the lack of air conditioning meant outdoor living and amusements in the summer. A more mischievous way to enjoy the sport involved spending an evening playing the game indoors, with empty Champagne bottles as stakes.

CHAMPAGNE COUPES

Also known as fingerbowl glasses—very Fitzgeraldian. Common Champagne flutes, by comparison, feel rather 1980s and invoke all sorts of *Working Girl* office party imagery.

Legend has it that the shape of the Champagne coupe glass was modeled on the breasts of Marie Antoinette or one of a variety of other French aristocrats, including Madame du Pompadour and Madame du Barry. At other times, the shape is attributed to Helen of Troy; supposedly her lover, Paris, made wax molds of the glorious breasts that "launched a thousand ships" and used the molds to make drinking glasses. None of these rumors is likely true, but who cares? The *idea* is enough: it emphasizes the sensuality with which fine Champagne should be consumed.

CHAMPAGNE-GLASS TOWERS

On the note of fingerbowl glasses, let's bring back Champagne-glass towers: a round pyramid of stacked coupes, in which Champagne is poured into the top glass and eventually trickles down to the ones on the lower tiers. Popular in the 1920s, such towers are the prettiest monuments to decadence.

CHAMPAGNE JELLY MOLDS

Jelly—i.e. gelatin—molds used to wobble with cheerful regularity on banquet tables. Among the most festive: ones that contained Champagne as the headlining ingredient; they also often sported strawberries, gooseberries, and raspberries in their shimmering golden bellies.

CHAMPAGNE MIDNIGHT SUPPERS

Throw one of these Champagne-drenched feasts—which begin at the stroke of midnight—to usher in your next birthday. Such fêtes should be reminiscent of society doyenne Caroline Astor's extravagant Gilded Age midnight suppers, in which she lavished hundreds of night-owl guests with bubbly and multiple courses following the latest masquerade in her famous ballroom.

ATLAS

Cocktail

❄ TO HELP YOU SHOULDER BURDENS ❄

Supporting the heavens on your shoulders might sound like
a rather presidential prestige job, but in Greek mythology,
the assignment was actually considered a punishment. In this
case, the condemned man was Atlas, a Titan who unwisely
rebelled against Zeus: always a no-no.

Sip his namesake cocktail to assist you in bearing your own
worldly burdens.

1 OUNCE APPLEJACK

½ OUNCE RUM

½ OUNCE COINTREAU

1 DASH ANGOSTURA BITTERS

ICE CUBES

---

*Shake with ice; strain through a back brace into
a chilled cocktail glass.*

Serves 1

ATTA BOY

Cocktail

This beverage can be administered to anyone in need of a little morale boost: Gulp one for courage before a big game, a lofty presentation, an inspiring oration, pre-Bar exam, pre-marriage proposal, and so on.

1½ OUNCES DRY GIN

¾ OUNCE FRENCH VERMOUTH

2 OR 3 DASHES GRENADINE

ICE CUBES

Shake with ice and strain into a chilled cocktail glass.
Serve with side of spinach, Wheaties, or other fortifying fare.

Serves 1

BALD HEAD

Cocktail

❄ TO CONSOLE ABOUT FOLLICULAR LOSS, ❄
REAL OR IMAGINED

This cocktail may have been named after Bald Head Island in North Carolina, but let's be juvenile and assume that it was created by a bartender with a glistening cranium.

Use this drink to provide comfort when your own fine head of hair is blowing away like the seeds of a late-summer dandelion. As you drain your glass, make sure to watch an old-guard flick exalting Men of Character Who Also Happen to Be Bald (like Yul Brynner in *The Magnificent Seven*, or any other of his films for that matter). A humorous alternative: Watch the *I Love Lucy* episode in which Lucy gives Ricky a vigorous home treatment for hair loss. When she was done with him, he likely could have used one of these.

½ OUNCE GIN

½ OUNCE FRENCH VERMOUTH

½ OUNCE ITALIAN VERMOUTH

1 DASH ABSINTHE

ICE CUBES

---

*Shake with ice and strain through a toupee into
a chilled cocktail glass.*

Serves 1

BATTERY CHARGER

Cooler

❄ THE ORIGINAL ENERGY DRINK ❄

Run down? Worn thin? Tuckered out? Forget Starbucks, and eschew Red Bull. What follows is the mid-century no-nonsense approach to resuscitation:

---

1 OUNCE PERNOD

¼ OUNCE GRENADINE

ICE CUBES

SELTZER

Pour Pernod and grenadine into a highball glass filled with ice; stir. Fill with seltzer (from an old-fashioned seltzer bottle, of course). You will be able to perform Herculean tasks within approximately three minutes of consuming.

Serves 1

THINK PINK

Although drinking was traditionally deemed a masculine occupation, an inordinate number of pink cocktails have been created over the years, perhaps in a bid to draw ladies to the bar. One of these drinks gets a delightfully scornful mention in the book *Auntie Mame* (1955):

> *"[Agnes] ordered something called a Pink Whiskers, which made the waiter blanch. [It] looked kind of nasty to me, but she sipped it ostentatiously, still wearing her gloves and with a great crooking of her little finger, and pronounced it extremely refreshing."*

Refreshing or nasty? Judge for yourself:

THE PINK WHISKERS COCKTAIL

¾ ounce apricot brandy
¾ ounce dry vermouth
2 dashes white crème de menthe
1 teaspoon grenadine
2 tablespoons orange juice
Ice cubes
1 ounce port

Combine all ingredients except the port in a cocktail shaker and shake vigorously. Strain into a cocktail glass. Delicately float the port on top.

⟶ SERVES 1 ⟵

Other blush-colored beverages from the past:

Pink Baby Cocktail	Pink Lady Cocktail
Pink Elephant Cocktail	Pink Lady Fizz
Pink Garter Cocktail	Pink Pearl Cocktail
Pink Gin Cocktail	Pink Rose Cocktail
Pink Goody Cocktail	Pink Squirrel Cocktail
	Pink Top Cocktail

BEE'S KNEES
Cocktail

❊ TO EXPRESS ADMIRATION ❊

Instead of sending a thank-you note, messenger someone a mason jar filled with the Bee's Knees Cocktail (as in, "You're the bee's knees—absolutely the best"). The 1920s offered up all sorts of these delightfully inane animal kingdom compliments, including:

"The Cat's Meow"
"The Cat's Pajamas"
"The Cat's Whiskers"
"The Duck's Quack"
"The Elephant's Instep"
"The Snake's Hips"

A sneaky little secret about this Prohibition favorite: The added teaspoon of honey supposedly masks the smell of the booze on one's breath.

---

1 TEASPOON FRESH LEMON JUICE

1 TEASPOON HONEY

½ OUNCE GIN

ICE CUBES

Shake with ice and strain into a chilled "elephant's instep."

Serves 1

BETWEEN-THE-SHEETS
Cocktail

❄ THE PERFECT NIGHTCAP FOR TWO ❄

The origin of this suggestively named cocktail is hotly contested, with several bartenders from various world capitals having claimed parentage. Some passionately believe that it was first poured in Harry's Bar in Paris; others would bet their firstborns that it was invented by a Mr. Polly, manager of the Berkeley Hotel, London, in 1921.

In any case, this sassy, pre–World War II favorite is the perfect pre-bedtime libation for two, either to help you both get your Zzzzs—or your jollies.

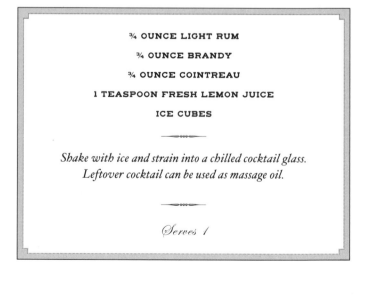

¾ OUNCE LIGHT RUM

¾ OUNCE BRANDY

¾ OUNCE COINTREAU

1 TEASPOON FRESH LEMON JUICE

ICE CUBES

*Shake with ice and strain into a chilled cocktail glass.
Leftover cocktail can be used as massage oil.*

Serves 1

LOVE POTIONS

VINTAGE DRINKS WITH SUGGESTIVE NAMES

Forget what's been written about bygone eras being prudish: If the following cocktail names—some of which date back to colonial times—are any indication of popular mindset, sex has *always* been on everyone's minds—and lips. Some of them are not exactly subtle, such as the "Bosom Caresser," which was so popular that it enjoyed a heap of variations. One version:

THE BOSOM CARESSER COCKTAIL

1 ounce brandy
1 ounce Madeira
1 dash grenadine
1 dash curaçao
1 egg yolk
Ice cubes

Shake with ice and strain into a cocktail glass.

→===   SERVES 1   ===←

Other libations with naughty connotations—at least within the context of today's vernacular:

Angel's Tit / *pg. 16*

Between-the-Sheets / *pg. 30*

Bosom

Climax

Hanky Panky / *pg. 83*

Nude Eel

Small Dinger

Spread-Eagle Punch (this name was likely more patriotic than dirty, but still worth including)

Symphony of Moist Joy / *pg. 182*

Turkish Harem

Up in Mabel's Room

Whoopee Highball

BIG BAD WOLF

Cocktail

Variations of the big bad wolf have appeared in folk and children's tales for hundreds of years: Aesop featured them prominently, as did the Grimm brothers. Practically *everyone* has heard Sergei Prokofiev's symphony and the tale of "Peter and the Wolf."

The story that you should keep in mind while serving the cocktail below: "The Three Little Pigs," in which a swaggering wolf menaces three sweet little piggies who've constructed houses from straw, sticks, and bricks respectively. Upon being barred entrance from each habitat, the wolf promises that he will "huff, and I'll puff, and I'll blow your house in."

We all know what happens to the pigs who lived in the straw and stick houses. But when the wolf swung around to the brick house, he couldn't blow it down, and had to resort to plunging down the chimney. Waiting for him in the hearth below: a pot of boiling water—and the third little pig enjoyed Wolf à la King that night for dinner.

Serve the old-fashioned Big Bad Wolf Cocktail to outsmartable, boastful bosses; braggart neighbors; and blusterers at large.

1 OUNCE BRANDY

½ OUNCE FRESH ORANGE JUICE

1 TEASPOON GRENADINE

1 EGG YOLK

ICE CUBES

*Shake with ice and strain into a chilled cocktail glass.
Serve with a side of ham.*

Serves 1

Serve alongside the

THREE LITTLE PIGS COCKTAIL

1 OUNCE GRENADINE

1 OUNCE WHISKEY

1 OUNCE GINGER ALE

ICE CUBES

Stir with ice and serve with squeals.

Serves 1

BISHOP

Cocktail

❄ TO BRING TO A CHURCH SUPPER ❄

History has provided many drink recipes for when you're in a holier-than-thou sort of mood (see the "Saints and Sinners" roster of biblically inspired cocktails, page 110). Yet this mid-nineteenth-century cocktail seemed particularly fetching, thanks to its mix of wholesome and sinful ingredients, and the instruction that it is "to be drunk while in a state of froth" (*Cooling Cups and Dainty Drinks*, 1869)—rather like a clergyman delivering an especially brimstone-filled sermon.

The recipe below makes enough for the whole congregation:

---

8 WELL-BEATEN EGGS

4 CUPS BOILING MILK

8 CUPS WHISKEY

SUGAR

1 DASH NUTMEG

10 CRUSHED CLOVES

Add the milk to the eggs, then stir in the whiskey.
Sweeten with sugar to taste; add the nutmeg and crushed cloves.
Think only pure thoughts while sipping.

Serves 20-25

BLOODHOUND

Cocktail

❊ TO HELP YOU RECOVER LOST OBJECTS ❊

This is essentially a strawberry Martini; it reached its height of popularity in the 1920s. Not only is the Bloodhound Cocktail the perfect summer drink, it also bestows upon its drinker the uncanny ability to locate misplaced keys, money-clips, grocery lists, lost loves, and the like.

1½ OUNCES GIN

¾ OUNCE DRY VERMOUTH

¾ OUNCE SWEET VERMOUTH

2 OR 3 CRUSHED STRAWBERRIES

ICE CUBES

FRESH STRAWBERRY FOR GARNISH

Shake with ice and strain into a chilled coupe Champagne glass. Garnish with a fresh strawberry and serve with an air of omniscience.

Serves 1

UNE GÉNÉRATION PERDUE

PARISIAN BARS PATRONIZED BY THE LOST GENERATION

Back in the 1920s, Gertrude Stein sat Ernest Hemingway down in her Paris salon and informed him that he was a member of a *génération perdue*:

"'That's what you are. That's what you all are,' Miss Stein said. 'All of you young people who served in the war. You are a lost generation.'

'Really?' [Hemingway] said.

'You are,' she insisted. 'You have no respect for anything. You drink yourselves to death.'"

Well, to be fair, if you were going to drink yourself to death, 1920s Paris was glamorous enough a place to do so. Here is a short list of Parisian bars and cafés closely associated with Hemingway, Fitzgerald, and other debauched Jazz Age expats; several of these establishments are still open today.

$\cdots$ $\cdots$

LA CLOSERIE DES LILAS

Long-gone patrons of this Montparnasse "lilac garden"—founded in 1847—included Miss Stein herself (and her lover, Alice B. Toklas), Henry James, Pablo Picasso, Lenin, and Trotsky. It is often said that Hemingway penned much of *The Sun Also Rises* at this café.

LE SELECT

Apparently when Hemingway and Picasso weren't at Closerie, they were here. Founded in 1923, the Select was open twenty-four hours a day and became wildly popular with the bohemian crowd. In

The Sun Also Rises, Lady Brett Ashley and Jake Barnes taxi to the café and they meet up with a "little Greek portrait painter whom everyone called Zizi" and a Count Mippipopolous, "who wore an elk's tooth on his watch-chain."

LES DEUX MAGOTS

The denizen of intellectuals and Surrealists, Les Deux Magots counted among its patrons Simone de Beauvoir, Françoise Giroud, Paul Morand, and Antoine de Saint-Exupéry. According to the restaurant, Jean-Paul Sartre "would take his seat at Les Deux Magots and write for hours, often without pause." Of course, Hemingway imbibed there too—but where *didn't* he drink?

HARRY'S NEW YORK BAR

Just over a century ago, a New York City–based bar was dismantled, shipped over to France, and reassembled in Paris. The resulting *boîte*—Harry's New York Bar—served up stiff drinks and American food to the usual suspects: Hem, F. Scott, and Miss Stein, among others.

"I had taken two finger-bowls of champagne, and the scene had changed before my eyes into something significant, elemental, and profound."

F. Scott Fitzgerald • THE GREAT GATSBY

BLUE BLAZER

Cocktail

Created circa 1850 by legendary bartender Jerry Thomas (see "An Ode to Professor Jerry Thomas," page 114, and "Knickerbocker Cocktail," page 104), it would be hard to overstate how famous this cocktail became in the second half of the nineteenth century. Supposedly a customer clomped into San Francisco's El Dorado gambling saloon, where Thomas tended bar, and shouted,

> *"Bar-keep! Fix me up some hell-fire that'll shake me right down to my gizzard."*

Thomas complied. After announcing to his bar patrons that they were about to witness the birth of a new beverage, he ignited the concoction that he'd whipped up. According to one history of the incident, "blue flame[s] shot toward the ceiling and ...Thomas hurled the blazing mixture back and forth between two mugs, with a rapidity and dexterity that were well nigh unbelievable."

Upon sampling the newly minted "Blue Blazer," the customer who'd demanded its creation "swayed in the wind," "shivered from head to foot," batted his eyes, and endured rattling teeth. Once these symptoms subsided, he cleared his throat and declared:

> *"He done it! Yes, sir, right down to my gizzard!"*

Revive the Blue Blazer to tempt the gizzards of your nearest and dearest when the next November fog rolls in.

2 HEATED MUGS

1 TEASPOON SUGAR

2½ OUNCES BOILING WATER

2½ OUNCES HEATED WHISKY

1 LEMON PEEL TWIST FOR GARNISH

———

In the first mug, dissolve the sugar in boiling water. In the other mug, pour the whisky and set it on fire. Pour the ingredients from one mug to another. As Thomas wrote in The Bon Vivant's Companion, *"If well done this will have the appearance of a continued stream of liquid fire." Pour the mixture into a heated wineglass and adorn with the lemon peel twist.*

Make sure that your home insurance policy is intact.

———

Serves 1

BROKEN SPUR

Cocktail

If cowboys rely on spurs to put a little *oomph* in their horses' get-along, then a broken spur implies an involuntary slowdown. In our never-slow-down contemporary world, which speeds up ever-faster by the millisecond, a vintage Broken Spur Cocktail might be *just* what we need.

---

1 OUNCE GIN

1 OUNCE WHITE PORT

1 DASH ANISETTE

1 EGG YOLK

ICE CUBES

——◆——

Shake with ice and strain into a chilled ten-gallon hat.

——◆——

Serves 1

GAG REFLEX

THE LEAST APPETIZING DRINK NAME IN HISTORY?

Let's just cut to the chase: Who in their right mind would *ever* order this drink? Unless he or she was trying to sabotage a blind date, *pronto*.

THE GINGIVITIS COCKTAIL

1 ounce gin
½ ounce grenadine
1 teaspoon cream
Ice cubes

Shake with ice and strain into a chilled cocktail glass. Garnish with a strand of dental floss.

⊹⊱⊰ **SERVES 1** ⊱⊰⊹

BULLSHOT

Cocktail

❄ TO CONSOLE YOU ON A DAMP NOVEMBER DAY ❄

Served warm, this old-fashioned drink is splendidly consoling on a wet autumn or winter day (a perfect "way to keep warm at a cold ballgame," advised legendary bartender Trader Vic). Long a staple of gentlemen's clubs, the Bullshot is a sophisticated version of the Bloody Mary, in which the tomato juice is swapped out for beef bouillon.

½ CUP BEEF BOUILLON

¼ OUNCE FRESH LEMON JUICE

1 TEASPOON WORCESTERSHIRE SAUCE

1 DASH TABASCO

A PINCH CAYENNE PEPPER

A PINCH SALT

2 OUNCES VODKA

1 LEMON SLICE FOR GARNISH

———

Combine all the ingredients except the vodka and lemon slice in a small pan and warm over medium heat, stirring constantly. Pour into a small mug over the vodka, mix with a spoon, and adorn with the lemon slice.

———

Serves 1

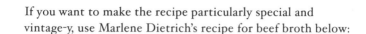

If you want to make the recipe particularly special and vintage-y, use Marlene Dietrich's recipe for beef broth below:

MARLENE DIETRICH'S BEEF TEA
(OR "LIQUID STEAKS")*

"4 pounds round steak cut into cubes; put into a mason jar. Heat the closed jar in a pot of water slowly, boiling for 4 hours. The liquid that you will find in the jar is enough food for a daily ration of a grown-up. Add salt and pepper [or] vegetable salt."

*Excerpted from *Marlene Dietrich's ABC* (1961)

CHANTICLEER

Cocktail

The word "chanticleer"—another term for rooster—has its roots in medieval fables, particularly Chaucer's "The Prologue of the Nun's Priest." This Canterbury Tale features a rooster named Chanticleer whose comb is "redder than fine coral, his beak is black as jet, his nails whiter than lilies, and his feathers shine like burnished gold." Naturally, Chanticleer is terribly vain and quite literally rules the roost.

Along slinks a fox who thinks that Chanticleer would make quite a tasty nibble. He flatters Chanticleer's singing so much that the rooster—bursting with pride—stretches his neck and crows loudly. The fox leaps forward, grabs him by the neck, and splits for the woods.

The moral of the story: never to trust a flatterer. Serve Chanticleer's namesake cocktail to anyone who meets this description, and let him know that you're on to his game.

"Any party stands or falls by the nature and excellence of its drinks. For all cocktails, economy is fatal."

Ethelind Fearson • *THE RELUCTANT HOSTESS* (1954)

1 OUNCE ORANGE GIN
OR ANOTHER LIGHT ORANGE LIQUEUR

1 OUNCE FRENCH VERMOUTH

1 EGG WHITE

———

Shake and strain into a cocktail glass.
The Old Waldorf-Astoria Bar Book *(1935) instructs*
readers to "Add a Cock's Comb if desired."

———

Serves 1

A HISTORICAL NOTE / In the mid-1800s, a newspaper suggested the
term "Chanticleer" as a more refined alternative to the word "cock tail,"
which it deemed vulgar. Clearly the motion was never carried.

WHAT'S IN A WORD?

THE MUDDLED ORIGIN AND VARIOUS MEANINGS OF THE WORD "COCKTAIL"

The term came into popular use in the nineteenth century, but language experts say that its origins are unclear. Of course, this doesn't prevent people from positing theories:

••• **SOME ARE CONVINCED** that an innkeeper named Betsy Flanagan is responsible for the word: She apparently used cock tail feathers as swizzle sticks when serving drinks during the American Revolution. (Her inn is variously placed in Virginia or Pennsylvania, depending on who's recounting the story.) According to one version of the tale, the spirited Ms. Flanagan roasted a rooster stolen from a Loyalist and festooned the accompanying drinks with the cock's feathers.

••• **ANOTHER CAMP ASSERTS** that the word stems from an old French recipe of mixed wines called *coquetel*, which may have been carried to America by General Gilbert du Motier Marquis de Lafayette in the late 1700s.

••• **OTHERS CLAIM** that "cocktail" comes from *cock tailings*, i.e., the dregs or "tailings" of spirits casks, which would be drained out through their spigots (also known as "cocks"), stirred together, and sold as a cheap beverage.

••• **ANOTHER THEORY:** The term arose from a West African word *kaketal* (scorpion). The drink may have borrowed its name from the scorpion-like sting it delivers.

What fewer people know: The word "cocktail" has a variety of delightful secondary meanings, including:

1 / A horse with a docked tail.

2 / A horse that is not a thoroughbred,
with unknown or mixed breeding.

3 / A man of little breeding who pretends
at being a gentleman.

CHARLIE CHAPLIN

Cocktail

While most of us have seen at least one Marx Brothers film, fewer have likely seen the work of Charlie Chaplin, one of the greatest stars of the silent film era.

Once ranked by the American Film Institute as one of the ten greatest male screen legends of all time, this comedic actor is perhaps best remembered for his role as the Tramp—a character that re-emerged in dozens of short- and feature-length films. Chaplin's Tramp was best described as a gentlemanly vagrant, who sported elegant but endearingly ill-fitting clothes, a derby hat, and a tidy mustache. When sound came to movies, Chaplin refused to make the Tramp speak on film; he finally retired the character in 1936 with the aptly named film *Modern Times*.

Serve Chaplin's pre–Prohibition-era cocktail—once a favorite at New York City's Waldorf-Astoria—when you need a break from the white noise of modern times. It's been proven to quiet even the most egregious of loud-talkers and monologuers.

¾ OUNCE FRESH LIME JUICE

¾ OUNCE GIN

¾ OUNCE APRICOT BRANDY

ICE CUBES

———

Shake with ice and strain into a chilled cocktail glass.
Garnish with a whangee cane.

———

Serves 1

"The problem with the world is that everyone is a few drinks behind."

Humphrey Bogart • ACTOR

CORPSE REVIVER
Cocktail

This drink will come in very handy when you need to find a deceased relation's lost insurance policy and the Ouija board is being unresponsive. Whip up a batch of the recipe below, and pour glasses of it onto the grave of the dearly departed (making sure that you employ a "one for you, one for me" policy as you go) until the promised revival takes place.

However, the Corpse Reviver recipe listed in *The Savoy Cocktail Book* (1930) comes with the caveat that "four of these taken in swift succession will unrevive the corpse again"—so work fast.

¾ OUNCE LILLET BLANC

¾ OUNCE COINTREAU

¾ OUNCE GIN

¾ OUNCE FRESH LEMON JUICE

1 DASH ABSINTHE

Stir well with a shovel and strain into a cocktail glass.

Serves 1

[PLATE II]

Corpse Reviver Cocktail

ALL THAT GLITTERS

DRINKS NAMED AFTER OLD HOLLYWOOD'S SILVER SCREEN GODDESSES

Back in the day, most of the film-going public could never have hoped for the privilege of kissing a glamorous movie star. The next best thing: sipping a cocktail named after one of these iconic beauties:

Ginger Rogers / *pg. 189*

Jean Harlow

Lupe Vélez

Mae West / *pg. 116*

Marlene Dietrich

Mary Pickford

Rosalind Russell

Perhaps the most amusingly named cocktail in this category: the **GARBO GARGLE**. It should be noted that when Garbo made the leap from silent star to talkie legend, her first spoken line was:

"Give me a whiskey, ginger ale on the side, and don't be stingy, baby." (*Anna Christie*, 1930)

....

THE GARBO GARGLE COCKTAIL

1 ounce brandy

¼ ounce fresh orange juice

¼ ounce grenadine

¼ ounce dry vermouth

1 dash crème de menthe

Ice cubes

1 dash port wine

Shake the brandy, orange juice, grenadine, vermouth, and crème de menthe with ice; strain into a chilled cocktail glass. Float the port on top.

SERVES 1

DAMN-THE-WEATHER

Cocktail

❄ FOR WHEN YOU'RE FEELING DEFIANT ❄

One can imagine Winston Churchill or Theodore Roosevelt uttering this phrase under adverse circumstances. Guzzle these cocktails to shore up your courage when you need to charge uphill—literally or figuratively—under perilous circumstances.

---

1 OUNCE GIN

½ OUNCE FRESH ORANGE JUICE

¼ OUNCE ITALIAN VERMOUTH

SEVERAL DASHES CURAÇAO

ICE CUBES

Shake with ice and strain into a bulletproof chilled cocktail glass.

Serves 1

"Always remember that I have taken more out of alcohol than alcohol has taken out of me."

Winston Churchill • FORMER BRITISH PRIME MINISTER

DANDY

Cocktail

The dandy—an endangered species—has the following definition:
"A man who is excessively concerned about his clothes and
appearance; a fop," but everyone knows that a dandy's pre-
occupation with beauty goes far beyond his garb. A dandy is
concerned with living Life as Art—as playwright, aesthete,
and dandy poster boy Oscar Wilde once wrote: "One should
either be a work of Art, or wear a work of Art." Additional
essential components of the dandy's persona: use of terribly
refined language, the cultivation of leisurely hobbies, and
the affectation of nonchalance.

Traditionally, a true dandy has also been obligated to plunge
himself into a gilt state of bankruptcy and die in the poor-
house, with only the memories of his glory days to sustain him.

The Dandy Cocktail is best enjoyed in palm-and-art-filled salons:

---

1 OUNCE RYE

1 OUNCE DUBONNET

1 TEASPOON COINTREAU

1 DASH ANGOSTURA BITTERS

1 PIECE LEMON PEEL

1 PIECE ORANGE PEEL

Stir with a walking stick and strain into a cocktail glass.
Garnish with a monocle and serve with a side of
withering witticisms.

Serves 1

DIPLOMAT

Cocktail

❊   TO IMPROVE YOUR INTERNATIONAL APPEAL   ❊

According to *Cocktails: How to Mix Them* (1922), this drink was "very well-known in the French Diplomatic Service"—and it likely sated countless FSOs from other nationalities as well.

Sip one to silkify your own skills of international negotiation. The French and Italian vermouths listed in the recipe will clearly make you particularly convincing to citizens of those respective countries:

⅔ OUNCE FRENCH VERMOUTH

⅓ OUNCE ITALIAN VERMOUTH

2 DASHES MARASCHINO LIQUEUR

ICE CUBES

1 MARASCHINO CHERRY FOR GARNISH

1 LEMON PEEL TWIST FOR GARNISH

———

Stir the vermouths and liqueur with ice and strain into a cocktail glass. Add the cherry and lemon twist, and sprinkle with state secrets.

———

Serves 1

DOLLY O'DARE

Cocktail

❅ TO FIGHT AGAINST CRIMINAL ELEMENTS ❅

Named after an obscure but intriguing mid-century comic book character, Dolly O'Dare earned her keep as a top sleuth for the police department, where she battled a criminal adversary called the Baron Blue.

Commemorate her contribution to the forces of good by resurrecting her namesake cocktail:

½ OUNCE DRY GIN

½ OUNCE FRENCH VERMOUTH

½ OUNCE APRICOT BRANDY

ICE CUBES

Shake with ice and strain into a chilled cocktail glass. Consume only in dark alleyways and abandoned, fog-wrapped docks.

Serves 1

THE FIZZ

Some drinks deserved to be relegated to the ashbin of history, but the refreshing, ebullient Fizz was not one of them. The perfect libation for the languorous dog days of summer—or celebrations during any season—the Fizz should be brought back right away.

Fizzes likely first appeared in the mid-nineteenth century: six recipes for these concoctions were included in *The Bon Vivant's Companion* (1862), the earliest cocktail book ever printed. They became hugely popular in New Orleans, whose Ramos Gin Fizz arguably rivaled the Mint Julep and Sazerac as the city's mascot cocktail.

What *is* a Fizz exactly? Once cited by legendary bartender Trader Vic as "an early-morning drink with a definite purpose—a panacea for hang-overs," the Fizz includes the following ingredients: liquor, lemon or lime juice, and sugar, which are shaken with ice, strained into a cocktail or Collins glass, and topped off with fizzing seltzer. Eggs are often added, cutting the sharp taste of the gin and citrus, and endowing the Fizz with a unique velvety-yet-light texture.

A "Silver Fizz" uses only egg whites; a "Golden Fizz" includes an egg yolk; and a "Royal Fizz" greedily incorporates a whole egg. And then, there is the queen of all Fizzes: the Diamond Fizz, which calls for Champagne instead of humble old seltzer. Resurrect the following recipe for your next fancy garden party:

....

THE RASPBERRY DIAMOND FIZZ

2 ounces gin
1 tablespoon raspberry liqueur
Juice from ½ lemon
1 egg white
8 fresh raspberries, quartered
Crushed ice
Champagne

Shake all ingredients except Champagne with plenty of crushed ice, strain into a chilled Champagne coupe, and top with a splash of Champagne.

SERVES 1

DU BARRY

Cocktail

This cocktail shares its name with Madame du Barry, who arguably rivals Cleopatra as the most famous mistress of all time. Born into less-than-regal circumstances as the illegitimate child of a seamstress, Madame du Barry later became a prostitute; she eventually managed to capture the affections of sexually voracious French King Louis XV. Swiftly rewarded for her efforts, she became one of France's wealthiest women under the patronage of her royal lover. Yet her story doesn't exactly have a fairytale ending: The "cake-eating" masses—unimpressed by her ascent—lopped off her head during the French Revolution.

Yet du Barry was great while she lasted. Next time you liaise with your undoubtedly equally talented mistress or illicit lover, mark the occasion with her namesake love potion:

---

1 OUNCE GIN

½ OUNCE FRENCH VERMOUTH

1 TEASPOON PERNOD

A DASH ANGOSTURA BITTERS

ICE CUBES

Stir with ice and strain into a chilled cocktail glass.
Garnish with a plush feather and a garter belt.

Serves 1

R-E-M-O-R-S-E

A POEM FROM *THE STAG'S HORNBOOK* (1918)

The cocktail is a pleasant drink,
It's mild and harmless, I don't think.
When you've had one, you call for two,
And then you don't care what you do.
Last night I hoisted twenty-three
Of these arrangements into me;
My wealth increased, I swelled with pride;
I was pickled, primed and ossified.
R E-M-O-R-S-E!
Those dry martinis did the work for me;
Last night at twelve I felt immense;
To-day I feel like thirty cents.
At four I sought my whirling bed,
At eight I woke with such a head!
It is no time for mirth or laughter—
The cold, grey dawn of the morning after.

EARTHQUAKE

Cocktail

❋ TO MAKE YOU INVULNERABLE TO DISASTER ❋

Next time tremors rumble along the fault line upon which your house is perched, reach for your cocktail shaker and the recipe below. As noted by *The Savoy Cocktail Book* (1930):

> "[The cocktail is] so-called because if there *should* happen to be an earthquake when you are drinking it, it won't matter."

Presumably it protects you in other similar natural (and unnatural) disasters as well.

½ OUNCE WHISKEY

½ OUNCE ABSINTHE

½ OUNCE GIN

ICE CUBES

———

Shake with ice, serve in a cocktail glass—and voilà!
Instant fallout shelter.

———

Serves 1

[PLATE III]

Earthquake Cocktail

ONE FOOT IN THE GRAVE

OLD-FASHIONED DRINKS FOR THE MORBID

Consistently gloomy? More gothic than Edgar Allan Poe? Don't fret: The bartenders of the past thoughtfully accommodated people of all dispositions. For the morose at heart, consult *The Savoy Cocktail Book*, first published in 1930, which cheerfully recommends the **THIRD RAIL COCKTAIL.** It's apparently "better than 11,000 volts":

THE THIRD RAIL COCKTAIL

½ ounce rum
½ ounce apple brandy
½ ounce brandy
1 teaspoon absinthe
Ice cubes

Shake with ice and strain into a chilled cocktail glass. Garnish with a plugged-in hairdryer.

⊰⊱ SERVES 1 ⊰⊱

Other "See You on the Other Side" concoctions include:

Corpse Reviver / *pg. 50*
Death in the Afternoon / *pg. 66*
Death in the Gulf Stream
Fare Thee Well

Hari Kari
Last Thought
Six Feet Under
Swan Song / *pg. 178*
Suicide

FANCY FREE
Cocktail

❄   FOR WHEN YOU'RE FEELING "ROMANCY"   ❄

This old-guard cocktail evokes the lyrics of "No Strings," the now-classic bachelor anthem sung by Fred Astaire in the 1935 film *Top Hat*:

> *No strings*
> *And no connection*
> *No ties to my affections*
> *I'm fancy free*
> *And free for anything fancy*

With his "decks cleared for action," Astaire's freedom makes him feel "romancy."

Modern imbibers of the drink commemorating this state of mind will instantly feel equally unmired and amorous.

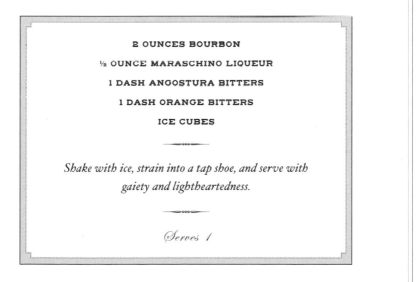

2 OUNCES BOURBON

½ OUNCE MARASCHINO LIQUEUR

1 DASH ANGOSTURA BITTERS

1 DASH ORANGE BITTERS

ICE CUBES

Shake with ice, strain into a tap shoe, and serve with gaiety and lightheartedness.

Serves 1

ALSO SEE / Top Hat Cocktail on page 188 and Ginger Rogers Cocktail on page 189.

FARE THEE WELL

— Cocktail —

❈ TO DULL THE HEARTACHE OF SAYING GOODBYE ❈

Heaven knows that poor Lord Byron might have appreciated some liquid consolation after separating from his wife, Annabelle; he wrote a poem titled "Fare Thee Well" (1816), which contained the following heart-wrenching stanza:

> *Fare thee well! thus disunited,*
> *Torn from every nearer tie,*
> *Sear'd in heart, and lone, and blighted,*
> *More than this I scarce can die.*

To assuage a similar separation anxiety, employ the following recipe:

---

1 OUNCE GIN

½ OUNCE SWEET VERMOUTH

½ OUNCE DRY VERMOUTH

½ TEASPOON CURAÇAO

ICE CUBES

Shake with ice and strain into a chilled cocktail glass
whose rim has been swirled in bittersweet memories.

Serves 1

FLOOR POLISH

Cocktail

❄ A CHEERFUL HOUSEKEEPING AID ❄

Either drink this concoction yourself to cheer you during
spring cleaning, or have it at the ready when your maid
arrives each week: It will make you as cheery as a 1950s
housewife.

---

1 OUNCE GIN

½ OUNCE DRY VERMOUTH

½ OUNCE SWEET VERMOUTH

1 OUNCE PINEAPPLE JUICE

ICE CUBES

---

*Shake with ice and strain into a mop bucket; swab floor
and repeat until a high sheen is achieved.*

Serves 1

NOTABLE DRINKS OF EPIC IMBIBER ERNEST HEMINGWAY

· · · —⟪⟫⟪⟫— · · ·

Ernest Hemingway once asserted that "a man does not exist until he is drunk." What follows is a short list of drinks popularly associated with the great author:

.... *Cocktail No. 1* ....

DEATH IN THE AFTERNOON

Named after Hemingway's 1932 book about bullfighting, the "Death in the Afternoon" cocktail was contributed by the writer to a 1935 collection of celebrity recipes. In it, he instructed brave souls to "*Pour one jigger of absinthe into a Champagne glass. Add iced Champagne until it attains the proper opalescent milkiness. Drink three to five of these slowly.*" Death in the afternoon, indeed.

.... *Cocktail No. 2* ....

THE MOJITO

This drink was reportedly invented at La Bodeguita del Medio in Havana, Cuba, where Hemingway—as a local resident—gulped them down regularly.

Ice cubes
6 ounces light rum
12 fresh mint sprigs
1 ounce lime juice
4 tablespoons sugar
Crushed ice
Club soda
Lime wedges for garnish

Place ice in shaker; add the rum, mint sprigs, lime juice, and sugar. Shake vigorously, and serve over crushed ice in a highball glass. Top off each glass with a splash of club soda and a lime wedge.

⊣⟫⟫ SERVES 4 ⟪⟪⊢

Cocktail No. 3

THE PAPA DOBLE

Some enthusiastic aficionados have asserted that Papa—as Hemingway was often called—invented the daiquiri. While this is unlikely, a particular variation bears his name: the "Papa Doble," or the Hemingway Daiquiri. According to legend, the author created the following recipe at Sloppy Joe's Bar in Key West: "*Mix 2 ounces of white or light rum, the juice from two limes, and the juice from half a grapefruit. Add a dash of Maraschino liqueur on the top, and serve it over crushed ice.*" Anyone who drinks a few of these will be seeing "doble" in no time.

FLU
Cocktail

❊ A ZIPPY ALTERNATIVE TO NYQUIL ❊

Everyone knows about the curative qualities of an old-fashioned hot toddy, but it's a pansy drink compared to the Flu Cocktail. This concoction—a favorite at The 19th Hole, a famous New York City speakeasy immortalized by caricaturist Al Hirshfeld—will absolutely slay any cold symptoms you might be harboring.

Or, at the very least, it will knock you out until the illness has run its course.

---

2 OUNCES RYE

1 TEASPOON GINGER BRANDY

1 TEASPOON FRESH LEMON JUICE

1 TEASPOON ROCK CANDY SYRUP

1 DASH GINGER EXTRACT

———

Stir and strain into a cocktail glass. Garnish with sniffles and consume with an air of woeful self-pity.

———

Serves 1

FLUFFY RUFFLES

Cocktail

❋ TO TRANSPORT YOU BACK TO TAP DANCE CLASSES ❋

This Prohibition-era favorite may have been named after an obscure musical that ran briefly in 1908. As a work of performance art, *Fluffy Ruffles* might have deserved its place in the ashbin of history, but the scrumptious lime-flavored cocktail sharing its title does not.

½ OUNCE RUM

½ OUNCE ITALIAN VERMOUTH

ICE CUBES

1 LIME OR LEMON PEEL FOR GARNISH

——◦◦◦◦——

Shake with ice and strain into a cocktail glass. Garnish with the lemon or lime peel; sip while humming "The Fluffy Ruffle Girls Rag" and doing a Broadway shuffle.

——◦◦◦◦——

Serves 1

FRANKENSTEIN

Cocktail

❄ FOR WHEN YOU'RE FEELING GOTHIC ❄

Frankenstein (1818) by Mary Shelley is generally considered to be a landmark work of romantic and gothic literature, and also a forerunner in the science fiction genre (also see H.G. Wells Cocktail, page 86). You probably know the story line: A scientist cobbles together a man from dead body parts (among other unspecified materials) and is rightly horrified by his creation—especially when the creature decides to rub out Frankenstein's family and friends, thus shrinking the list of people likely to give the scientist birthday and Christmas presents.

Despite its surprisingly cheery ingredients, Frankenstein's namesake cocktail is obviously best enjoyed in an atmosphere of degeneration, fear, and decay.

½ OUNCE DRY VERMOUTH

½ OUNCE GIN

¼ OUNCE APRICOT BRANDY

¼ OUNCE COINTREAU

Stir with "bones from charnel-houses" and strain into a chilled cocktail glass. Garnish with a "profane finger."

Serves 1

A RIVALRY COMMEMORATED

Few figures in New York City's history figure as prominently as Caroline Astor—the onetime self-appointed arbiter of America's Gilded Age society—who once asserted that only four hundred families met the criteria for membership in the city's elite social echelons. This just happened to be the capacity of her private ballroom, and she guarded access to this realm with the ferocity of Cerberus.

Then along came the Vanderbilts, whose wealth was a generation newer than that of the Astor clan. Mrs. Astor considered this family to be a horde of nouveau riche climbers to be fended off with every weapon in her arsenal—and a great American rivalry was formed.

At your next hoity-toity affair, serve both the Astor Cocktail and the Vanderbilt Cocktail.

ASTOR COCKTAIL

2 ounces gin
1 teaspoon fresh orange juice
1 teaspoon fresh lemon juice
Ice cubes

Stir with ice and strain into a chilled cocktail glass. Serve swathed in a beaver pelt

VANDERBILT COCKTAIL

1 ounce cherry brandy
1½ ounces brandy
2 dashes simple syrup
2 dashes Angostura bitters

Shake and strain into a cocktail glass. Garnish with a railroad spike.

⇥⇥ EACH SERVES 1 ⇤⇤

FROTH BLOWER
Cocktail

✳ FOR WHEN YOU'RE FEELING CHARITABLE ✳

At first glance, one might assume that "Froth Blowers" would be rather frivolous creatures; however, historically speaking, it appears that these creatures devoted themselves to some serious tasks. In the UK, during the 1920s, an organization calling itself the "Ancient Order of Froth Blowers" was established to raise funds for various charities. It wasn't all stern do-gooding, however: There appears to have been a boisterous imbibing element to the organization as well (hence the name, which evokes the blowing of froth off the top of a pint of ale).

In a pamphlet, the A.O.F.B. members described their outfit:

> *"A sociable and law abiding fraternity of absorbitive Britons who sedately consume and quietly enjoy with commendable regularity and frequention the truly British malted beverage as did their forbears and as Britons ever will, and be damned to all pussyfoot hornswogglers from overseas and including low brows, teetotalers and MP's and not excluding nosey parkers, mock religious busy bodies and suburban fool hens all of which are structurally solid bone from the chin up."*

The cocktail bearing the same name has nothing to do with the "truly British malted beverage" described, but it will still immediately make you want to contribute to the March of Dimes right away.

2 OUNCES GIN

1 TEASPOON GRENADINE

1 EGG WHITE

ICE CUBES

Shake vigorously with ice, strain into a chilled cocktail glass, and sip while reading the memoirs of Mother Teresa.

Serves 1

GOAT'S DELIGHT

Cocktail

Who doesn't like a goat? Even the Devil is fond of them, for goodness sake; as described by master storyteller Natalie Babbit, the Devil "always has one or another somewhere about, kept on as sort of a pet . . . [he] likes them so much [because] goats are one hundred percent unsentimental."

To be fair, the goat for which this cocktail was originally named was likely a human goat (a tertiary definition of the word includes "A lecherous man"). *The Old Waldorf-Astoria Bar Book* (1935) informs its readers that "As to who was the original 'goat' cheered by this cup, records are at least vague."

Still, it's more fun to imagine a delighted *animal* goat as you drink this cocktail.

¾ OUNCE BRANDY

¾ OUNCE KIRSCHWASSER

½ TEASPOON CREAM

1 DASH PERNOD

1 DASH ORGEAT (ALMOND-FLAVORED) SYRUP

ICE CUBES

———

Stir with ice using a pitchfork, and strain into a chilled cocktail glass. Garnish with strands of hay.

———

Serves 1

[PLATE IV]

Goat's Delight Cocktail

COCKTAIL CORNUCOPIA

————◦◦◦ **THE ART OF FROSTED FRUIT** ◦◦◦————

When you serve your next round of summer cobblers (see page 142) or set out a bowl of summer punch, forgo boring old chunks of ice and swap in frosted peaches, pears, cherries, berries, grapes, and plums—whatever fruit you fancy.

This suggestion comes courtesy of a Mrs. Marion W. Flexner, author of *Cocktail-Supper Cookbook* (1955), who implores her readers to place unwrapped, unpeeled fruit on a tray or "a piece of foil covered cardboard" in the freezer for about two hours. When removed from the freezer, "as soon as air strikes the fruit, it acquires a flattering coat of bloom," she promises. Place the fruit in the punch bowl or cocktail glasses immediately.

Served in a glistening silver punch bowl, such an arrangement makes a spectacular centerpiece.

GLOOM LIFTER
Cocktail

❊ TO CHASE AWAY THE MEAN REDS ❊

Not to be confused with plain old blues, for which nearly any old form of booze will suffice. The mean reds, as described by *Breakfast at Tiffany's* heroine Holly Golightly, are far worse:

> *"The blues are because you're getting fat or maybe it's been raining too long. You're sad, that's all. But the mean reds are horrible. You're afraid and you sweat like hell, but you don't know what you're afraid of."*

The only things that assuaged Holly's angst was a trip to Tiffany & Co., of course—but if you're not in striking distance of the jewelry franchise, a Gloom Lifter will do the trick too.

1½ OUNCES IRISH WHISKEY

½ TEASPOON BRANDY

½ TEASPOON SUGAR

1 EGG WHITE

JUICE FROM ½ LEMON

1 DASH RASPBERRY SYRUP

1 DASH GRENADINE

ICE CUBES

Shake with ice and strain into a large chilled cocktail glass. If gloom does not abate, chase with a Gloom Raiser Cocktail and then a Gloom Chaser until mean reds subside.

Serves 1

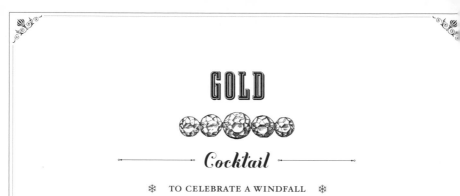

GOLD

Cocktail

❋ TO CELEBRATE A WINDFALL ❋

Within a few years of the fateful 1848 discovery of gold in northern California, hundreds of thousands of gold-diggers had flocked to the territory-turned-state, and gold worth billions of dollars in today's money had been yanked out of the ground. America went gold-crazy, and bars across the nation were often frontline recipients of newly found wealth.

The bar of the once-lavish and now-extinct original Waldorf-Astoria Hotel (which was supplanted by the Empire State Building) was no exception; it created a Gold Cocktail named "after the product of 'them thar hills,' finders of which came to the Bar in great numbers."

Revive its recipe to celebrate any jackpot moments in your own life.

½ OUNCE GIN

½ OUNCE ITALIAN VERMOUTH

1 DASH ORANGE BITTERS

———

Stir with a pick-ax, strain through a screen, and serve in a miner's pan.

———

Serves 1

THE GREAT ZIEGFELD

Cocktail

This drink is named for legendary showman Florenz Ziegfeld, the force of nature behind the Ziegfeld Follies. These lavish, wildly creative Broadway revue productions—which ran from 1907 to 1931—are likely most remembered today for the beautiful, extravagantly clad chorus girls, nicknamed the "Ziegfeld girls."

One of the most famous Ziegfeld starlets, Billie Burke, did Ziegfeld the favor of becoming his wife; she then did *us* the favor of preserving his favorite concoction for posterity. The recipe follows, in narrative form from Mrs. Ziegfeld:

> *"[Ziggy] used to prepare 2/3 gin and 1/3 pineapple juice, with the rim of the glass moistened in lemon juice or lime and then twirled in powdered sugar, served very cold. At least he always twirled the first two or three in powdered sugar. After that, it didn't matter."*

GREEN-EYED MONSTER
Cocktail

❄ TO SERVE TO A JEALOUS FRENEMY ❄

It's a rather erudite way to one-up an envious acquaintance discreetly; after all, the phrase "green-eyed monster" was coined by Shakespeare and uttered by Iago in *Othello*:

> *O, beware, my lord, of jealousy;*
> *It is the green-ey'd monster, which doth mock*
> *The meat it feeds on.*

A repulsive modern version calls for buckets of Everclear alcohol, Mountain Dew, and pineapple juice, but the past offers a more refined recipe:

½ OUNCE IRISH WHISKEY

½ OUNCE ITALIAN VERMOUTH

½ OUNCE PERNOD

1 DASH ANGOSTURA BITTERS

ICE CUBES

——————

Shake with ice and strain into a chilled cocktail glass.
Reserve enough to spill into the crotch of the imbiber—
accidentally, of course.

——————

Serves 1

COMPARATIVE DRUNKENNESS

Over the years, the intoxicated have been compared to some rather unlikely creatures, objects, and personae. For example, circa 1386, Chaucer used the phrase "dronke … as a Mous" (apparently that epoch's mice had the unfortunate habit of plunging into beer vats). Another still-used phrase—"drunk as a lord"—emerged in the 1600s, and may allude to the fact that in those days noblemen could afford to drink more than commoners, and regularly overindulged to prove the point.

Some amusing/bemusing historical expressions of comparative drunkenness:

Drunk as a beggar

Drunk as a billy goat

Drunk as a boiled owl

Drunk as a brewer's horse

Drunk as a broom

Drunk as dancing pigs

Drunk as a devil

Drunk as a drowned rat

Drunk as a Dutchman

Drunk as a fiddler

Drunk as a hog / sow / swine / pig

Drunk as a monkey

Drunk as a nurse at christening

Drunk as a poet

Drunk as a pope

Drunk as a sailor

Drunk as a skunk

Drunk as a wheelbarrow

[PLATE V]

Hanky Panky Cocktail

HANKY PANKY

Cocktail

Invented in London by the Savoy Hotel bar's earliest mistress—
Ada Coleman—this cocktail was named by Sir Charles Hawtrey
(a clever chap who just happened to be Noël Coward's mentor).
Ms. Coleman described the drink's genesis to a newspaper
in 1925:

> *"Charles . . . was one of the best judges of cocktails that I knew.*
> *Some years ago, when he was overworking, he used to come into*
> *the bar and say, 'Coley, I am tired. Give me something with a bit*
> *of punch in it.' It was for him that I spent hours experimenting*
> *until I had invented a new cocktail. The next time he came in,*
> *I told him I had a new drink for him. He sipped it, and, draining*
> *the glass, he said, 'By Jove! That is the real hanky-panky!' And*
> *Hanky-Panky it has been called ever since."*

But we can assume that it re-earned its name many times over,
thanks to all of the naughty behavior it has surely inspired in
its devotees.

---

1 OUNCE ITALIAN VERMOUTH

1 OUNCE DRY GIN

2 DASHES FERNET-BRANCA

ICE CUBES

1 ORANGE PEEL TWIST FOR GARNISH

Shake with ice and strain over ice into a highball glass.
Garnish with the orange peel twist and serve with a spanking.

Serves 1

DAMN THE TORPEDOES

HISTORICAL DRINKS WITH
WAR-ORIENTED NAMES

War and drinking go hand in hand. We drink to get through wars; we drink to get over them; and *then* we drink as we strategize the next military entanglement.

A list of old-guard cocktails for the bellicose:

Army Cocktail

Artillery Cocktail

Blood and Sand Cocktail

Captain's Blood Cocktail

Death in the Afternoon Cocktail / *pg. 66*

Death in the Gulf Stream Cocktail

Depth Bomb Cocktail

Guided Missile Cocktail

Platoon Cocktail

Retreat from Moscow Cocktail

Shrapnel Cocktail

T.N.T. Cocktail / *pg. 184*

Torpedo Cocktail

War Days Cocktail

HELL

Cocktail

❄ **AN EARLY RESPONDER IN HELLISH SITUATIONS** ❄

Serve this admittedly bizarre, old-fashioned concoction
immediately upon signs of:

1 / Arrival of jury duty summons

2 / Arrival of audit from the I.R.S.

3 / Nearing of any sort of destiny-determining test

4 / Implosion of home sewage system

5 / Post-traumatic stress induced by irreparable
bad haircut

¾ OUNCE BRANDY

¾ OUNCE CRÈME DE MENTHE

ICE CUBES

1 PINCH RED PEPPER

———

Shake with ice and strain into a chilled cocktail glass;
sprinkle with red pepper before serving. Drink until your
hair grows out or the case is dismissed.

———

Serves 1

H.G. WELLS

Cocktail

❉ TO BE TRANSPORTED TO ANOTHER WORLD ❉

Not that H. G. Wells (often called the "Father of Science Fiction") ever needed any assistance transporting his readers. For example, on October 30, 1938, millions of listeners heard radio news alerts of a violent Martian attack on Earth; many ran out of their homes screaming while others packed up their cars and fled. What they were *really* hearing: Orson Welles's radio adaptation of H.G. Wells's iconic novel *The War of the Worlds*.

This mid-century recipe is strong enough to be used as fuel for the rockets sometimes featured in Wells's writings:

---

1 OUNCE BOURBON

½ OUNCE DRY VERMOUTH

1 DASH PERNOD

ICE CUBES

1 LEMON PEEL TWIST FOR GARNISH

———

Stir with ice and strain into a chilled cocktail glass.
Garnish with the lemon peel twist and a spritz of misanthropy.

———

Serves 1

HIGH HAT

Cocktail

In bygone eras, to "give someone the high-hat" meant to treat him condescendingly, just as a "high-hatted" person was a snob. Serve the High Hat Cocktail at a party to turn it into an exceedingly haughty event (it will positively *reek* of the royal enclosure at Royal Ascot in no time).

Alternatively, if you are a guest at such an affair, and are not particularly happy about being there, you can set up shop near the bar and slug down these surprisingly refreshing drinkies to help you muddle through.

¾ OUNCE BRANDY

¾ OUNCE FRESH GRAPEFRUIT JUICE

½ TEASPOON SIMPLE SYRUP

ICE CUBES

Shake with ice and strain into a chilled hand-cut crystal cocktail glass.

Discard—with great disdain—any ingredients not handled with white gloves.

Serves 1

SO HAPPY TOGETHER

OLD-FASHIONED DRINKS THAT GO HAND IN HAND

Inseparable Combination No. 1

DUKE COCKTAIL

1 egg
½ ounce Cointreau
¼ ounce fresh orange juice
½ ounce fresh lemon juice
¼ ounce maraschino liqueur
Ice cubes

Shake with ice and strain into a polo helmet, and top off with Champagne.

&

DUCHESS COCKTAIL

½ ounce Pernod
½ ounce sweet vermouth
½ ounce dry vermouth

Shake with iced emeralds and strain into a large glass.

EACH SERVES 1

Inseparable Combination No. 2

EVERYTHING BUT COCKTAIL

¾ ounce gin
¾ ounce bourbon
¼ ounce apricot brandy
¾ ounce fresh lemon juice
¾ ounce fresh orange juice
1 egg
¾ tsp sugar

Shake in an iced cocktail shaker and strain into an absolutely enormous cocktail glass. Garnish with a rubber band ball, a sprinkling of paper clips, and any other random objects found in your junk drawer.

&

KITCHEN-SINK COCKTAIL

Same as above, substituting rye for bourbon. The latter will be noticeably sweeter.

EACH SERVES 1

Inseparable Combination No. 3

HARVARD COCKTAIL

¾ ounce brandy
¾ ounce sweet vermouth
2 dashes Angostura bitters
1 teaspoon simple syrup
Ice cubes

Shake with ice and strain into a chilled cocktail glass. Serve alongside a Hasty Pudding.

&

PRINCETON COCKTAIL *(One variation thereof)*

1½ ounces gin
2 dashes of orange bitters
Ice cubes
1 ounce port

Shake the gin and bitters with ice; strain into a chilled cocktail glass; add the port last. Garnish with a tiger's tooth and serve with a heavy course load.

&

YALE COCKTAIL

1½ ounces gin
¾ ounce dry vermouth
1 dash maraschino liqueur
1 teaspoon simple syrup
2 dashes orange bitters
Ice cubes

Stir with ice, skulls, and bones, and strain into a chilled cocktail glass.

EACH SERVES 1

Inseparable Combination No. 4

GODFATHER COCKTAIL

1 ounce Scotch whisky
1 ounce amaretto

Stir with a crowbar and strain into a chilled cocktail glass.

&

GODMOTHER COCKTAIL

1 ounce vodka
1 ounce amaretto
Ice cubes

Stir with ice, strain into a chilled cocktail glass, and serve with list of wishes to be granted.

EACH SERVES 1

"HOOP LA!"

Cocktail

❄ TO CREATE A COMMOTION ❄

Definitions for the word "hoopla" include "sensational publicity" or "bustling excitement or activity; commotion." Equally delightful, old-fashioned synonyms: hullabaloo, brouhaha, and ballyhoo.

The basis for the "Hoop La!" recipe below comes to us—complete with quotations and exclamation point—courtesy of the old Savoy Hotel, which presumably saw quite a bit of hullabaloo and brouhahas over the years. Consuming this beverage—a cousin to the Sidecar—will immediately encourage you to create a ruckus, distraction, or hubbub.

½ OUNCE FRESH LEMON JUICE

½ OUNCE LILLET BLANC

½ OUNCE COINTREAU

½ OUNCE BRANDY OR COGNAC

ICE CUBES

Shake with ice, strain into a chilled cocktail glass, and serve while in a state of frenzied excitement.

Serves 1

HORSE'S NECK

Cocktail

❄ TO ACCESSORIZE YOUR JODHPURS ❄

This was apparently a booze-free drink when it first became popular in the late nineteenth century, consisting of a mild combination of ginger ale, lemon peel, and ice. Yet somebody figured out that it tasted better with bourbon; the new-and-improved version was requested by the updated name "Horse's Neck with a Kick." Serve it at your next Kentucky Derby party, or bring a thermos of it to the races.

---

1 FULL LEMON PEEL CUT INTO A SPIRAL

ICE CUBES

2 OUNCES BRANDY

1 OR 2 DASHES ANGOSTURA BITTERS

GINGER ALE

Place the peel in a highball glass; make sure the end hangs over the edge of the glass. Fill it with ice. Add the brandy and bitters, and fill the rest of the glass with ginger ale. True aficionados drink it from a dressage boot.

Serves 1

Another 1932 recipe—courtesy of the bartender of New York City's Prohibition-era Ship Ahoy speakeasy—calls for a teaspoon of sugar and a "glass of gin," to be topped with ginger ale.

THE CRUSTA

"An improvement on the cocktail," declared iconic bartender Jerry Thomas (see "An Ode to Professor Jerry Thomas" on page 114), who defined the Crusta as a fancy cocktail with a small piece of ice and some lemon juice added. Nearly a century later, bartending legend Trader Vic added that a drink could only be considered a "legitimate" Crusta if it involved "a frosted wineglass and the entire peeling of a lemon or orange fitted right into the glass."

The peeling of the fruit in one aesthetically pleasing piece is naturally the most challenging aspect of re-creating a Crusta. But if you have a steady hand and are feeling ambitious, here's a recipe for a brandy version:

THE BRANDY CRUSTA

¼ ounce fresh lemon juice, plus extra for coating the glass's rim

Powdered sugar

1 lemon for peeling

1½ ounces brandy

½ ounce curaçao

2 dashes Angostura bitters

2 dashes maraschino liqueur

Ice cubes

Chill one wineglass and frost it by dipping the rim first in fresh lemon juice and then swirling it in powdered sugar. Somehow manage to peel a whole lemon in one piece; slide the peel into the wineglass, making sure that it stays below the sugared rim. In his version of this recipe, Trader Vic sternly instructs his readers to "cover the entire inside of the glass [with the peel]." Shake the remaining ingredients with ice and pour carefully into the prepared glass.

SERVES 1

INCOME TAX

Cocktail

For millennia, death and taxes have been the only certainties in life. Happily, bartenders of yore have both categories covered. For the first, they created cocktail fare such as the Six Feet Under, the Suicide, the Last Thought, and so on (see "One Foot in the Grave: Old-Fashioned Drinks for the Morbid," page 62).

For the latter category, revive the following recipe on Tax Day. It is appropriately strong for the occasion—and also has a cheering splash of zesty orange.

---

1 OUNCE GIN

¼ OUNCE FRENCH VERMOUTH

¼ OUNCE ITALIAN VERMOUTH

1 DASH ANGOSTURA BITTERS

JUICE FROM ¼ ORANGE

ICE CUBES

1 ORANGE PEEL TWIST FOR GARNISH

Shake with ice and strain into a chilled cocktail glass.
Garnish with the orange peel twist, a calculator,
and a small noose.

Serves 1

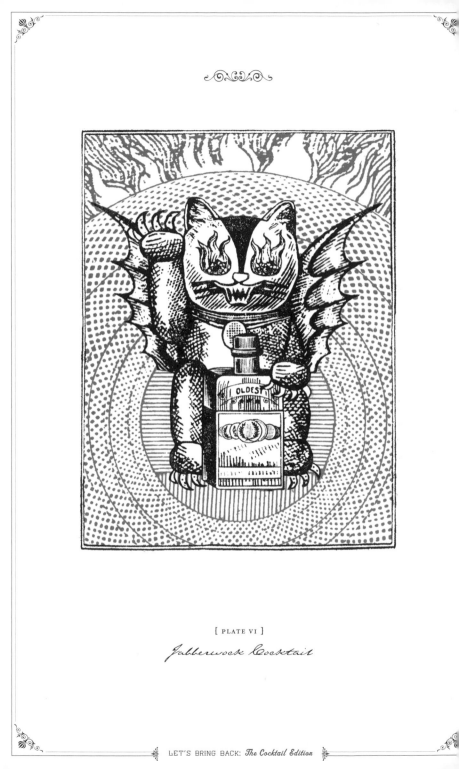

[PLATE VI]

Jabberwock Cocktail

JABBERWOCK

Cocktail

You'll surely recall the fearful Jabberwock conjured up in Lewis Carroll's *Through the Looking-Glass and What Alice Found There* (1872), with its "jaws that bite," "claws that catch," and "eyes of flame." For generations, its eponymous cocktail has either tamed one's inner beast—or taunted it. You stand warned.

The original recipe calls for Caperitif, which is no longer manufactured; swap in Lillet Blanc or Dubonnet instead.

½ OUNCE GIN

½ OUNCE DRY SHERRY

½ OUNCE LILLET BLANC OR DUBONNET

1 DASH ORANGE BITTERS

ICE CUBES

Stir with ice using a vorpal sword and galumph into a chilled cocktail glass.

Serves 1

JUNE BRIDE

Cocktail

With her pre-wedding jitters, literary iconess and June bride Daisy Buchanan of *The Great Gatsby* likely could have used a few of these. Instead, she got "drunk as a monkey" courtesy of a bottle of Sauternes on the eve of her betrothal:

> "'Gratulate me,' she muttered. 'Never had a drink before, but oh how I do enjoy it . . . Tell 'em all Daisy's change' her mine. Say: "Daisy's change' her mine!"'"

It is simply good common sense for any maid of honor to have the following vintage cocktail handy (along with spirits of ammonia and a cold compress), lest she face the unenviable task of hooking a skittish June bride into her white gown.

1½ OUNCES GIN

½ EGG WHITE

½ TEASPOON FRESH LEMON JUICE

½ TEASPOON SUPERFINE SUGAR

2 DASHES LIQUEUR OF CHOICE

ICE CUBES

---

*Shake with ice and strain into a very big chilled cocktail glass.
Serve with a pre-nup.*

Serves 1

PUNCH DRUNK

Punch bowls are the Lolitas of serving ware: filled with pink party punch, they look dainty and sweet and innocent, but portend all sorts of naughty behavior. They used to be the heart and soul of the party; now hardly anyone has them in their cupboards anymore. Fashionable since the 1600s, they've only recently fallen out of vogue for some unfathomable reason.

In you're wondering what constitutes a punch, here's some help from a 1757 ode to punch, attributed to Bostonian Samuel Mather:

> *You know from Eastern India came*
> *The skill of making punch as did the name*
> *And as the name consists of letters five,*
> *By five ingredients is it kept alive.*

The word "punch" was derived from the Sanskrit *pancha*, which meant "five"—and in those days, the five ingredients included tea (paticularly green), arrack (an alcohol made from coconut flowers, sugarcane, or grain in Southeast Asia), sugar, lemons, and water. Teas—particularly green teas—were often also added to the concoctions.

Some of the more memorably named punches due for a revival:

Bengal Lancers' Punch	Scorpion Punch
Chickadee Punch	Shark's Tooth Punch
Fish House Punch	Stag Special Punch
Kill Devil Punch / *pg. 100*	Tip-Top Punch
Knickerbocker Punch	Whirligig Punch
Mother's Ruin Punch	Zombie Punch / *pg. 199*

JUNGLE FIRE
Sling

Sadly, there are no fires involved in the making of this mid-century cocktail (see the Blue Blazer, page 38, to satisfy any pyro-libation cravings)—but if you wanted to extend the Jungle Fire Sling's name into a party theme, the possibilities are endless. Strew tangles of jungle vines across the floor and periodically set things aflame throughout the evening. Your guests will never forget it.

---

1 OUNCE CHERRY BRANDY

1 OUNCE BRANDY

½ OUNCE BENEDICTINE

½ OUNCE PARFAIT D'AMOUR

SHAVED ICE

GINGER ALE

———

*Stir the brandy and liqueur with a spear, pour into
a tall glass filled with shaved ice, and top off with ginger ale.
Garnish with a sprinkling of giant ants.*

———

Serves 1

KICKING COW

Cocktail

Our forebears considered breakfast time to be a perfectly appropriate cocktail hour (see "Hair of the Dog: Socially Acceptable Morning Cocktails," page 169). The following mid-century drink—served at the Stork Club, among other *boîtes*—makes an excellent alternative to syrup-drenched pancakes when you're feeling too lazy to make the batter:

> ⅔ **OUNCE WHISKEY**
>
> ⅓ **OUNCE MAPLE SYRUP**
>
> ⅓ **OUNCE CREAM**
>
> **ICE CUBES**
>
> ———
>
> *Shake with ice and strain into a chilled cereal bowl.*
> *Best consumed in front of Saturday morning*
> *television cartoons.*
>
> ———
>
> *Serves 1*

KILL DEVIL

Punch

In the late 1600s, thanks to the introduction of trade with the West Indies, rum made its appearance on the shores of New England. Described in the parlance of the day as "that cussed liquor" or "Rumbullion alias Kill Divil—a hot hellish and terrible liquor," it became incredibly popular with the colonial crowd; by 1728, more than two million gallons had been imported. It was only a matter of time until "Kill Divil" found its way into a punch bowl.

Below is an adaptation of an eighteenth-century rum punch; keep it handy in case any wayward spirits or demons make their way into your home.

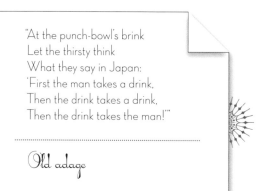

"At the punch-bowl's brink
Let the thirsty think
What they say in Japan:
'First the man takes a drink,
Then the drink takes a drink,
Then the drink takes the man!'"

....

Old adage

ONE 750-ML BOTTLE COLD CHAMPAGNE

1½ CUPS LIGHT RUM

JUICE OF 1 LEMON

2 CUPS BREWED GREEN TEA

SUGAR OR SIMPLE SYRUP

CAKE OF ICE

Mix the first three ingredients together; add in the green tea and sugar. Pour into a punch bowl containing a cake of ice, and store in your refrigerator until serving. Ladle out quickly in the case of any head-spinning or speaking-in-tongues.

Serves 10

KING'S RUIN

Cocktail

A sneaky way to take advantage of your royal competitors: Ply them with this cocktail, and you'll be able to outwit them in no time. It apparently earned its name because in the old days, few monarchs could resist it; many of the "old, bearded kings of Europe who used to frequent Foyot's, the Café de Paris, Maxim's, and the Ritz" counted the King's Ruin as a favorite libation, according to Stork Club chronicler Lucius Beebe.

1½ CUPS ICED CHAMPAGNE

2 OUNCES GOOD COGNAC

ICE CUBES

1 LEMON PEEL TWIST FOR GARNISH

—

*Pour into a tall Collins glass with 1 or 2 cubes of ice.
Garnish with lemon peel twist and serve swaddled in ermine.*

—

Serves 1

LIQUID ASSETS

History's bartenders created a bevy of transporting drinks for millionaires—actual and aspiring. From a certain point of view, they made access to wealth relatively democratic: For a buck, anyone could buy an "Emerald," or spend some time in the presence of an English king, an Indian prince, or a Wall Street robber baron.

· · · ⟋⟍⟋⟍⟋⟍ · · ·

KNICKERBOCKER
Cocktail

A Dutch surname sported by some of New York's earliest colonists, the word "Knickerbocker" has since become a widely recognized emblem of the great city. In fact, the cocktail bearing the name is still served and consumed zealously at the famous, grand Knickerbocker Club (known affectionately by its gentlemen members as the "Knick") on Manhattan's Upper East Side, and should be more widely reintroduced to the rest of the world.

What follows is an 1862 recipe by America's so-called Father of Mixology, Jerry Thomas, who categorized the Knickerbocker as a "Fancy Drink" rather than a "Cocktail." One sip will cart you back to the (very) sweet old days.

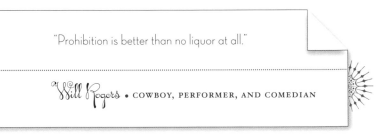

"Prohibition is better than no liquor at all."

Will Rogers • COWBOY, PERFORMER, AND COMEDIAN

½ LIME, OR LEMON; SQUEEZE OUT THE JUICE,
AND PUT THE RIND AND JUICE INTO THE GLASS

2 TEASPOONFULS OF RASPBERRY SYRUP

1 WINEGLASS (4 OUNCES) SANTA CRUZ RUM

½ TEASPOON OF CURAÇAO

SHAVED ICE

BERRIES FOR GARNISH

———

*Shake well with ice and strain into a chilled cocktail glass.
Garnish with berries in season. If this is still not sweet enough
for you, pour out the cocktail and drink straight from
the bottle of raspberry syrup.*

———

Serves 1

BACCHANALIAN BROUHAHAS

WINE DRINKS OF ANCIENT ROME

· · · ────── · · ·

While it would be nice to have the Roman gods in our lives again (they were always up to something inspiringly naughty), it's questionable whether the wines of the ancient Romans would appeal to modern tastes. They often had to dilute their wines with water (and sometimes seawater), sweeten them with honey, and temper them with lemon juice and spices—just to get them to the point of palatability. What a shame that Bacchus never got to experience a simple, lovely glass of Cabernet Sauvignon.

Yet if you decide to stage an ancient Roman orgy of some variety, here's a modern re-creation of the sweet Roman drink *mulsum*, a mixture of wine and honey.

ANCIENT ROMAN MULSUM

Warm ½ cup clear honey. Add one bottle of medium-dry white wine and stir. Chill before serving.

─────── SERVES 4–5 ───────

"Wine [is] a constant proof that God loves us, and loves to see us happy."

Benjamin Franklin • STATESMAN, DIPLOMAT, INVENTOR, AND AMERICAN FOUNDING FATHER

LANDLADY

Cocktail

When you've blown the month's rent on a pair of red-soled stilettos or a new golf club, and the landlady comes knocking, be prepared. Sit her down on the sofa, inquire after her health and family, compliment her frock, and ply her with several glasses of the vintage cocktail detailed below. A rent extension will materialize in no time.

---

1 OUNCE GIN

1 TEASPOON GRENADINE

½ EGG WHITE

ICE CUBES

———

Shake with ice and strain into a chilled cocktail glass.
Serve with lots of solicitous, apologetic smiles and nods.

———

Serves 1

LAUGHING SOUP

Cocktail

Down this drink upon discovering that you've burned the roast, overcooked the chicken, or scalded the soup (or, as in the case of a certain Author Who Shall Remain Anonymous, managed unwittingly to cook a stainless-steel spoon in a vat of squash soup for two hours). It makes a nice laugh-it-off preamble to the ensuing restaurant dinner, or companion beverage to the pizza you order instead.

---

1 OUNCE GIN

½ OUNCE FRENCH VERMOUTH

½ TEASPOON FRESH LEMON JUICE

½ TEASPOON POWDERED SUGAR

ICE CUBES

Shake with ice and strain into a chilled cocktail glass.
Serve with a good, old-fashioned, reliable frozen dinner.

Serves 1

LAWYER'S REVENGE

Cocktail

❊ FOR WHEN YOU'RE FEELING LITIGIOUS ❊

This old-guard drink will be useful whether the lawyer in question is avenging on your behalf (to put additional fire in your belly and aid the Great Cause), or directing his or her wrath *at* you (courage-provider/coping mechanism).

½ OUNCE REGULAR WATER

¼ TEASPOON SUGAR

1 PIECE ORANGE PEEL

ICE CUBES

1 OUNCE PORT WINE

1 DASH VICHY WATER

Combine the sugar and the orange peel with the regular water and mix well. Pour this over ice in a Collins glass, and add the wine. Add a dash of Vichy and a snippet of oratory swagger.

Serves 1

Other trial-related cocktails to keep the Lawyer's Revenge company:

Crook Cocktail	Straight Law Cocktail
Defender Cocktail	Third Degree Cocktail
Judge Cocktail	

SAINTS AND SINNERS

BYGONE COCKTAILS WITH
RELIGIOUS UNDERTONES

The story of the tangled relationship between temptation and resistance, indulgence and penitence, is one of the oldest in the book. Here is a short list of cocktails that positively brim with hellfire and holiness:

The Abbey Cocktail
Angel Cocktail
Archbishop Punch
Beadle Cocktail
Bishop Cocktail / *pg. 34*
Bishop's Cooler
Cardinal Cocktail
Christ Cocktail
Church Parade Cocktail
Churchwarden Cocktail
Devil's Cocktail
Devil's Leap Cocktail
Devil's Tail Cocktail
Eve's Garden Cocktail
Fallen Angel Cocktail

Fig Leaf Cocktail
Garden of Eden Cocktail
Hell Cocktail / *pg. 85*
Pope Cocktail
Puritan Cocktail
St. Francis Cocktail
St. John Cocktail
St. Peter Cocktail
Satan Cocktail
Satan's Whiskers Cocktail
    (straight) / *pg. 167*
Satan's Whiskers Cocktail
    (curly) / *pg. 167*
Temptation Cocktail
Vesper Cocktail

LEAVE-IT-TO-ME

Cocktail

❄ A BRAVADO ENHANCER ❄

This must-bring-back early twentieth-century mixed drink serves two ever-relevant purposes:

1 / To put you in a take-charge mood when a difficult task needs doing and everyone else around you is an idiot,

or,

2 / To convince someone to leave you a desired object or raft of funds in his or her Last Will and Testament. Note that some of the ingredients are appropriately sugary to help you sweeten your case.

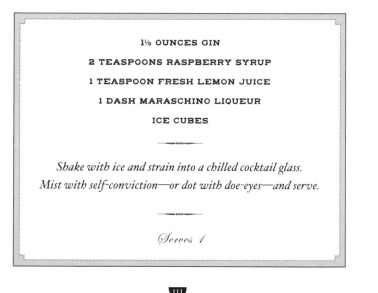

1½ OUNCES GIN

2 TEASPOONS RASPBERRY SYRUP

1 TEASPOON FRESH LEMON JUICE

1 DASH MARASCHINO LIQUEUR

ICE CUBES

Shake with ice and strain into a chilled cocktail glass.
Mist with self-conviction—or dot with doe-eyes—and serve.

Serves 1

[PLATE VII]

Loud-speaker Cocktail

LOUD-SPEAKER
Cocktail

❄ TO HELP MAKE YOURSELF HEARD ❄

Apparently the Loud-Speaker Cocktail has long been on hand to assist those with meek speaking habits or enunciation issues. Many voice-reliant professionals have used it as a lubricating crutch, according to *The Savoy Cocktail Book* (1930), which asserts:

> "[The Loud-speaker] gives to Radio Announcers their peculiar enunciation. Three of them will produce oscillation, and after five it is possible to reach the osculation stage."

Daily consumption of this cocktail will immediately render your vowels crisp, your voice distinctive, and give you a ringing projection. Plus, it's cost efficient as well, compared to the services of an elocution expert.

½ OUNCE DRY GIN

½ OUNCE BRANDY

¼ OUNCE COINTREAU

¼ OUNCE FRESH LEMON JUICE

ICE CUBES

———

Shake with ice and strain into a chilled cocktail glass. Gargle several times daily to achieve maximum loud-mouth effect.

———

Serves 1

AN ODE TO PROFESSOR JERRY THOMAS

AMERICA'S "FATHER OF MIXOLOGY"

In 1862, Jerry Thomas published *The Bon Vivant's Companion ... or ... How to Mix Drinks*, the first cocktail book to be issued in America. In an introduction to a 1928 edition of the landmark tome, writer Herbert Asbury described its author in the following way:

> "Briefly, Jerry Thomas was a bartender. But *what* a bartender! His name should not be mentioned in the same breath with that of the frowsy gorilla who, in these dark days of Prohibition, may be found lounging behind the bar of a dingy basement speakeasy."

Indeed, far from an unkempt monkey, "Professor" Thomas, as he was nicknamed, was an "imposing and lordly figure of a man . . . possessed of immense dignity." Visitors to his famed post in the El Dorado gambling saloon in San Francisco encountered a man sporting a spotless white jacket, a diamond-festooned shirt front, and an impressive walrus mustache—or so the legend goes. As the *New York Times* would later say of Thomas: "Like Davy Crockett, Daniel Boone, and Buffalo Bill Cody, he was the sort of self-invented, semi-mythic figure that America seemed to spawn in great numbers during its rude adolescence."

Dandyish adornments aside, Thomas took the business of mixing drinks very seriously and pioneered a variety of concoctions that became national sensations (see the Blue Blazer Cocktail, page 38, and the Knickerbocker Cocktail, page 104). He even embarked on an international tour, reportedly towing with him a glistening set of solid-silver bar utensils worth $4,000 and astounding "the effete drinkers of the Old World with . . . his virtuosity," according to Asbury.

His successors have bowed at his altar for generations; *The Savoy Cocktail Book* (1930) calls him "the greatest Bartender of the Past." Let us continue to *salaam*.

MAE WEST

Cocktail

❄ FOR WHEN YOU'RE FEELING BAWDY ❄

Widely regarded as Old Hollywood's Queen of Sassy One-Liners, Ms. West (1893–1980) managed to get herself banned from NBC Radio after a scandalous, double-entendre-laden guest appearance in 1937. Many young people today would recognize her famous quips, but are less likely to be familiar with the woman who uttered them:

> *"I used to be Snow White, but I drifted."*

> *"Too much of a good thing can be wonderful."*

> *"A hard man is good to find."*

> *"When I'm good, I'm very good—but when I'm bad, I'm better."*

> *"Good girls go to heaven. Bad girls go everywhere else."*

> *"When women go wrong, men go right after them."*

> *"I've been in more laps than a napkin."*

When you next find yourself in a ribald mood, honor her memory by sipping this namesake cocktail. Note that it's flavored with an appropriate punch of cayenne pepper.

1 OUNCE BRANDY

½ EGG YOLK

½ TEASPOON SUGAR

ICE CUBES

1 DASH CAYENNE PEPPER

Shake the brandy, egg yolk, and sugar with ice and strain into a chilled cocktail glass. Add the dash of cayenne pepper and a dollop of naughtiness.

Serves 1

MAIDEN'S BLUSH

Cocktail

❄ FOR DEMURE LASSES ❄

Ladies: Whether you genuinely *are* demure or are attempting to *seem* demure, the old-fashioned Maiden's Blush Cocktail will bestow upon you the qualities of shyness, modesty, and reserve. An excellent complement to a pastel chiffon dress and a lily of the valley corsage.

1½ OUNCES GIN

2 TEASPOONS GRENADINE

2 TEASPOONS CURAÇAO

1 DASH FRESH LEMON JUICE

ICE CUBES

---

*Stir with ice, strain into a chilled cocktail glass,
and serve with suppressed giggles.*

Serves 1

COME HELL OR HIGH WATER

WEATHER- OR NATURAL-DISASTER-EVOKING LIBATIONS

History's bartenders commemorated nature in all of her states. When the sun pierced through the clouds, they were on hand with the "Sunshine Cocktail." When it poured, they handed you a "Cloudy with Showers." Hurricanes gave people an excuse to empty out everything in their liquor cabinets, or to head to the nearest grand hotel bar to ride out the storm in style (and not surprisingly, a "Hurricane Cocktail" adorned countless early- and mid-century bar cocktail menus).

Some vintage weather-inspired potations:

Cloudy Sky Rickey

Cloudy with Showers Cocktail

Damn-the-Weather
Cocktail / *pg. 53*

Earthquake Cocktail / *pg. 60*

Fair and Warmer Cocktail

Fair Weather Cocktail

Heat Wave Drink

Hurricane Cocktail

Hurricane Punch

London Fog Cocktail / *pg. 169*

Sunshine Cocktail

Thunder Cocktail

Thunder and Lightning Cocktail

Thunderclap Cocktail

Weather-Be-Damned Cocktail

Whispers of the Frost Cocktail

MONKEY GLAND

Cocktail

❄ AN UNLIKELY FOUNTAIN OF YOUTH ❄

The name of this drink has been making people blanch and/or snicker for nearly 100 years. Invented in Paris in the 1920s, it referenced the work of Dr. Serge Voronoff, who grafted monkey testicles onto the testicles of men in an effort to combat signs of aging. While Dr. Voronoff denied that the precious monkey glands functioned primarily as an aphrodisiac, the masses assumed that the glands would turn their new owners into King Kongs in the sack; men lined up out the door and around the block to undergo the procedure.

The experiments caused an international sensation (poet e.e. cummings wrote of "that famous doctor who inserts monkey-glands in millionaires"), and various bartenders claimed to have been the first to create a cocktail commemorating the glandular vogue.

---

2 OUNCES DRY GIN

1 OUNCE FRESH ORANGE JUICE

2 DASHES GRENADINE

1 DASH ABSINTHE

ICE CUBES

———

Shake with ice and strain into a chilled cocktail glass.
Sip, grip a mirror, and watch your wrinkles
and sags melt away.

———

Serves 1.

[PLATE VIII]

Monkey Gland Cocktail

MOTHER-IN-LAW

Cocktail

❋ FOR WHEN YOU'RE FEELING SPITEFUL ❋

This hilarious recipe was uncovered in the rather ancient cocktail book *Cooling Cups and Dainty Drinks* (1869). You can serve it to the mother of your husband or wife and smolder with impish satisfaction as she sips it—or guzzle it yourself to recover from the latest obligatory visit.

---

1 PART OLD ALE

1 PART BITTER ALE

———

Mix and pour.

MY OWN

Cocktail

※ FOR WHEN YOU'RE FEELING UTTERLY POSSESSIVE ※

One of the most boring lessons of growing up: learning to share. People who come from large families with heaps of possession-sharing siblings will appreciate this vintage cocktail. Make sure to prepare it while hidden in a closet or squirreled away in a locked bathroom. If discovered, clutch the glass and shaker to your chest, and offer none to anyone else.

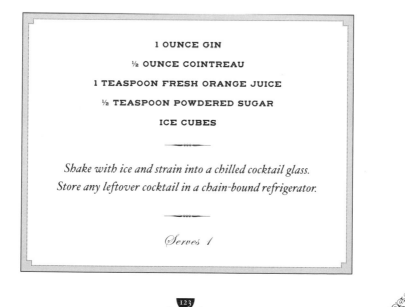

1 OUNCE GIN

½ OUNCE COINTREAU

1 TEASPOON FRESH ORANGE JUICE

½ TEASPOON POWDERED SUGAR

ICE CUBES

Shake with ice and strain into a chilled cocktail glass.
Store any leftover cocktail in a chain-bound refrigerator.

Serves 1

[PLATE IX]

90 Degrees in the Shade Cocktail

90 DEGREES IN THE SHADE

Cocktail

❊ FOR THE DOG DAYS OF SUMMER ❊

After all, when it gets *that* hot outside, what else is there to do but lie in the shade of a magnolia tree, fan yourself while reading Faulkner, and drink yourself into a pleasant stupor? The "lemon ice" in this variation adds a delightful element of childhood innocence to this whiskey-and-soda recipe:

CLUB SODA

2 OUNCES LEMON ICE OR LEMON SORBET

2 OUNCES WHISKEY

Put the club soda into the freezer until ice flecks just begin to form in the bottle. Place the lemon ice in a Collins glass; pour in the whiskey and top with the iced club soda. Accessorize with a hand-held fan and an air of languor.

Serves 1

"Civilization begins with distillation."

William Faulkner • AUTHOR

NINOTCHKA

Cocktail

Once again, you've been accused of being humorless, a wet blanket, a moping Eeyore.

Take solace: Many glamorous people have found themselves in the same pickle—including the great Greta Garbo, whose legendary onscreen world-weariness eventually began to drag on her box-office ratings as well. Hollywood execs decided to shine a ray of light into the Garbo gloom by releasing the 1939 film *Ninotchka*, her first comedy—and such a stark departure from her previous roles that the publicity campaign's tagline was, "Garbo laughs!" People around the world flocked to theaters to behold the upturned corners of Garbo's mouth.

Like Garbo, you can prove to your naysayers that you're not a stick in the mud: After downing several Ninotchkas, you're guaranteed to transform into a one-man vaudeville show.

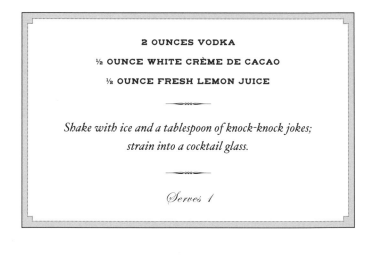

2 OUNCES VODKA

½ OUNCE WHITE CRÈME DE CACAO

½ OUNCE FRESH LEMON JUICE

Shake with ice and a tablespoon of knock-knock jokes;
strain into a cocktail glass.

Serves 1

ROSE-LIPPED MAIDENS

OLD-FASHIONED COCKTAILS
CELEBRATING THE MOUTH

EXALTING PEARLY WHITES

Broadway Smile Fancy Drink | Royal Smile Cocktail
Prince's Smile Cocktail | Smiler Cocktail

EXALTING KISSES

Angel's Kiss Fancy Drink | Last Kiss Cocktail
Hobson's Kiss Mixed Drink | Soul Kiss Cocktail
Kiss Cocktail | Sour Kisses Cocktail
Kiss from Heaven Cocktail | Stolen Kisses Cocktail / *pg. 176*
Kiss-Me-Quick Fancy Drink | Widow's Kiss Cocktail / *pg. 153*

EXALTING BREATH

Panther's Breath Cocktail / *pg. 130* | Sheik's Breath Cocktail / *pg. 171*

OLD SALEM
Smash

❊ FOR WHEN YOU'RE FEELING WITCHY ❊

Most of us associate the Salem of yore with a certain nasty spate of witch trials in the late 1600s, but the town was renowned for other things as well, as this splendid old-guard refreshment shows. One can almost see ole' Abigail Williams and Betty Parris secretly sipping these behind the barn after a hard day of finger-pointing.

---

2 TABLESPOONS SUGAR

2 TABLESPOONS WATER

4 SPRIGS FRESH MINT

½ GLASS SHAVED ICE

2 OUNCES DARK RUM

———

Put the sugar into a tall glass and add the water.
Add the mint, the shaved ice, and rum, then mix well.
A large-volume recipe can also be made in an
iron cauldron and mixed with a broom.

———

Serves 1

OYSTER

Cocktail

✳   TO SHOW THAT YOU'VE ARRIVED   ✳

Some sources say that this drink originated as a San Francisco delicacy in the 1860s, where it was allegedly favored by just-struck-it-rich California gold miners who considered oysters to be edible status symbols (*see also*: Gold Cocktail on page 80). After all, didn't oysters appear on the menus of the East Coast's most hoity-toity restaurants?

Originally, the Oyster Cocktail apparently did not contain alcohol, as demonstrated in this 1895 recipe from *Modern American Drinks: How to Mix and Serve All Kinds of Cups and Drinks*:

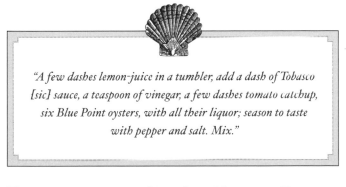

"A few dashes lemon-juice in a tumbler, add a dash of Tobasco [sic] sauce, a teaspoon of vinegar, a few dashes tomato catchup, six Blue Point oysters, with all their liquor; season to taste with pepper and salt. Mix."

The concoction was served in a glass with a spoon. However, later aficionados took the Oyster Cocktail from a G-rating to adult status by adding an ounce or two of vodka to the recipe.

Remember to make this drink yourself when you eventually catch up with the Joneses.

PANTHER'S BREATH
Cocktail

❋ AN ALTERNATIVE TO BREATH MINTS ❋

According to one source, the breath of the panther was once considered "a sweet odour, as if it were a mixture of every perfume." If that is the case, the cocktail detailed below should be on offer in any and every contained, crowded space (i.e. elevators, subway cars, etc.) in which the bad breath of your neighbors is a menace.

½ OUNCE CURAÇAO

½ OUNCE CREAM

1 DROP ANGOSTURA BITTERS

———

Pour the curaçao into a chilled sherry or cocktail glass; float the cream on top. Add the drop of bitters, and serve. Sip before making any amorous moves on a first date.

———

Serves 1

PARISIEN

Cocktail

France's *Belle Epoque* (or "Beautiful Era") period lasted from the late nineteenth century until World War I. When you are in the mood to swap out status updates, digitally downloaded music, and McDonald's for brilliant cabaret theater, opera gloves, and Champagne-soaked dinners at Maxim's, sip one of these shimmeringly decadent concoctions.

A member of the pousse-café family (in which each ingredient is added from densest to the least dense to achieve a layered effect), the Parisien Cocktail should be sipped (preferably through a sterling silver or gold straw) one liqueur at a time.

¼ **OUNCE FRAMBOISE**

¼ **OUNCE MARASCHINO LIQUEUR**

¼ **OUNCE CURAÇAO**

¼ **OUNCE GREEN CHARTREUSE**

¼ **OUNCE CHAMPAGNE**

With a steady hand, pour the ingredients carefully into a chilled pousse-café glass in the order listed, making sure that they don't mix. Best when shared with a demimondaine.

Serves 1

PARKEROO

Cocktail

The old-fashioned Parkeroo Cocktail will become an invaluable component in your tool shed. After all, as Parkeroo creator Willard Parker once noted:

> "While painting a picket fence around my house, I discovered that after two Parkeroos I could remain standing and let the fence revolve around the brush."

If only Tom Sawyer had known about it!

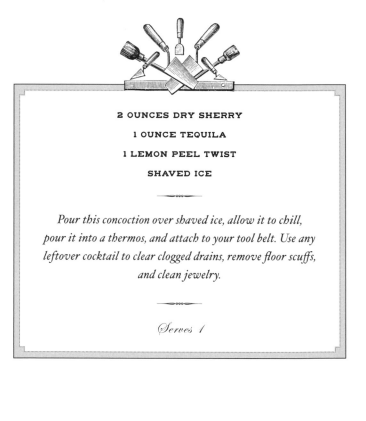

2 OUNCES DRY SHERRY

1 OUNCE TEQUILA

1 LEMON PEEL TWIST

SHAVED ICE

Pour this concoction over shaved ice, allow it to chill, pour it into a thermos, and attach to your tool belt. Use any leftover cocktail to clear clogged drains, remove floor scuffs, and clean jewelry.

Serves 1

THE CUP

A satisfying beverage made from iced wine and fruit. Said *The Old Waldorf-Astoria Bar Book* (1935), "In olden times, vegetables were also included, particularly cucumbers." In England, the refreshing Pimm's Cup—usually garnished with cucumber and bits of cut-up fruit—remains something of a national emblem, and is even downed between sets of civilized grass-court tennis matches.

For more formal occasions, bring back the sophisticated Claret Cup, featuring red wine from the Bordeaux region of France. The recipe below will fill a punch bowl and serve at least ten people.

CLARET CUP

2 tablespoons sugar

¼ cup water

One 750-ml bottle Claret

2 ounces brandy

1½ ounces Benedictine

1½ ounces maraschino liqueur

One 33.8-ounce bottle of seltzer

Lemon and orange slices or frosted fruit

Combine the sugar and water in a small saucepan; bring to a boil, reduce heat to low, and simmer for five minutes. Set aside to cool. In a large punch bowl, mix together the wine, brandy, Benedictine, maraschino liqueur, and cooled sugar water. Cover and refrigerate. To serve, pour in the seltzer, and decorate with either the lemon and orange slices or the frosted fruit (see "Cocktail Cornucopia: The Art of Frosted Fruit" on page 76).

SERVES 10

PASSENGER LIST
Cocktail

❄ TO HELP YOU SAIL AWAY ❄

It would have been sublime to sip one of these while coasting across the Atlantic between New York and England in a magnificent 1930s Cunard liner with all of the fixings: bon voyage parties, cabin-warming parties, flowers sent to cabins, black-tie dinners, invitations to sit at the captain's table, and ballroom dancing.

The next best thing: sipping one of these vintage cocktails while watching old films about romantic transatlantic crossings, such as:

Shall We Dance (1937) with Fred Astaire and Ginger Rogers

An Affair to Remember (1957) with Cary Grant and Deborah Kerr

A Night at the Opera (1935) with the Marx Brothers

Gentlemen Prefer Blondes (1953) with Marilyn Monroe

Sabrina (1954) with Audrey Hepburn

The Lady Eve (1941) with Barbara Stanwyck and Henry Fonda

A mid-century version of the Passenger List Cocktail:

½ OUNCE BRANDY

½ OUNCE DRY GIN

½ OUNCE PARFAIT D'AMOUR

½ OUNCE YELLOW CHARTREUSE

1 DASH PERNOD

ICE CUBES

*Shake with ice and strain into a chilled cocktail glass.
Use this beverage for a bon voyage toast, preferably
while perched dockside upon your exquisite stack of Goyard
traveling trunks.*

Serves 1

"Though wars are fought, famines endured, monarchs overthrown, it is the givers of pleasure, the bringers of beauty, the gay at heart who endure. These are history's darlings."

Elsa Maxwell • HOSTESS, AUTHOR, AND GOSSIP COLUMNIST

ALL THE BETTER TO SEE YOU WITH

—◦○○ **OLD-FANGLED DRINKS NAMED** ○○◦—
AFTER BODY PARTS

In the film *Out of Africa* (1985), Robert Redford (as Denys Finch Hatton) notes how many poems have been devoted to celebrating different parts of human anatomy. "Lips, eyes, hands, face . . . hair, breasts . . . legs, arms, even the knees," he muses. "But not one verse for the poor foot."

History's mixologists have been no less attentive to the body—and unlike their poet counterparts, at least one of them *did* manage to create a cocktail containing the word "foot":

TANGLEFOOT COCKTAIL

1 ounce Bacardi rum
1 ounce Swedish punsch
½ ounce orange juice
½ ounce lemon juice
Ice cubes

Shake with ice and strain into a chilled cocktail glass.

⊷⊷ **SERVES I** ⊷⊷

Other physique-referencing libations:

Angel's Lips Cocktail
Angel's Tit Cocktail / *pg. 16*
Baby's Fingers Cocktail
Baby Titty
Bald Head Cocktail / *pg. 26*
Bosom Cocktail

Beauty Spot Cocktail
Glad Eye Cocktail
Lady Fingers Cocktail
Maiden's Hair Cocktail
Tiptoes Cocktail
Twinkle Toes Cocktail

PLATINUM BLONDE

Cocktail

❄   TO EVOKE YOUR INNER MARILYN MONROE   ❄

Whether you're too lazy to touch up your roots or simply want to find out if gentlemen really do prefer blondes, this vintage cocktail will spare you a trip to the salon.

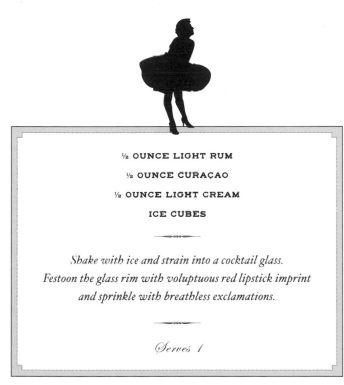

½ **OUNCE LIGHT RUM**

½ **OUNCE CURAÇAO**

½ **OUNCE LIGHT CREAM**

ICE CUBES

Shake with ice and strain into a cocktail glass.
Festoon the glass rim with voluptuous red lipstick imprint
and sprinkle with breathless exclamations.

Serves 1

[PLATE X]

Poet's Dream Cocktail

POET'S DREAM

Cocktail

❊ **FOR A LITERARY SLUMBER** ❊

This old-guard cocktail sounds perfectly romantic at first—after all, might it not be named for the work of English poet Percy Bysshe Shelley?

"The Poet's Dream" (1875)

On a Poet's lips I slept
Dreaming like a love-adept
In the sound his breathing kept;
Nor seeks nor finds he mortal blisses,
But feeds on the aerial kisses
Of shapes that haunt Thought's wildernesses [...]

One hopes this is the case, as it would likely be far less pleasant to be trapped in the dream of Allen Ginsberg:

"Howl" (1956)

I saw the best minds of my generation destroyed by madness,
starving hysterical naked, [...]

CONTINUED ON NEXT PAGE ⫸→

Either way, sipping one before bedtime will surely have you dreaming in iambic pentameter:

½ OUNCE GIN

½ OUNCE FRENCH VERMOUTH

½ OUNCE BENEDICTINE

ICE CUBES

1 LEMON PEEL TWIST FOR GARNISH

—————

Shake with ice and strain into a chilled cocktail glass.
Adorn with the lemon peel twist.
An optional addition: 2 dashes orange bitters
and a handful of adjectives.

—————

Serves 1

"Candy
Is dandy
But liquor
Is quicker."

Ogden Nash

HOW I LEARNED TO STOP WORRYING AND LOVE THE BOMB

THE MILTOWN COCKTAILS

In the 1950s, screen siren Marilyn Monroe pronounced that diamonds were a girl's best friend—but the more ubiquitous accessory of the era was the Miltown, a tiny white tranquilizer pill. Those babies were everywhere, and *everyone* tried to profit from the phenomenon. *The Age of Anxiety*, a book documenting America's post-H-bomb fears, reports that in the mid-1950s even Tiffany & Co. cashed in, doing "brisk sales of 'ruby-and-diamond-studded pill coffers for those who wished to glorify their new-found happiness.'"

Since pills and booze have often gone hand-in-hand in fashionable society, it was fairly inevitable that the chicly anxious would create a Miltown Cocktail. The most popular version consisted of vodka, tomato juice, and a single Miltown pill.

A second variation known as the Guided Missile ("popular among the late-night crowd on the Sunset Strip," noted one historian) contained two shots of vodka and two Miltowns.

Perhaps the most outrageous offering of the genre: the Miltini, a dry martini in which a Miltown wallowed in the bottom of the glass instead of an olive.

THE COBBLER

A drink served in a tall glass, filled with shaved or cracked ice, fruit, and liquor. "A swell drink to coast on," commented Trader Vic in his 1947 *Bartender's Guide*.

Serve the following old-guard Champagne Cobbler to celebrate a summer birthday or anniversary:

....

CHAMPAGNE COBBLER

Cracked or shaved ice

¼ ounce fresh lemon juice

¼ ounce curaçao

Champagne

1 orange slice for garnish

1 pineapple slice for garnish

Fill a tumbler halfway with cracked or shaved ice; add the lemon juice and curaçao. Top with Champagne and stir. Garnish with the orange and pineapple slices.

⟻⟫⟩⟩ **SERVES 1** ⟨⟨⟪⟼

....

POLLYANNA

Cocktail

❋   TO GIVE YOU A JOLT OF OPTIMISM   ❋

The old-fashioned term "Pollyanna" refers to "a person who is constantly or excessively optimistic," inspired by the title character in a best-selling 1913 novel by Eleanor Porter. In this book, Pollyanna's philosophy of life centers on what she chirpily calls "The Glad Game," which consists of finding something to be glad about in every situation, no matter how dire. For example, when stashed in an attic by a dour aunt, Pollyanna delights in the view from her perch. *Nothing* gets this dame down—not even a car accident that breaks both of her legs. (Pollyanna's take on that situation: Well, I'm glad that I *had* legs that worked, at least.)

The ingredients in her namesake cocktail are in equal parts delusion-inspiringly strong and girlishly sweet.

---

3 SLICES ORANGE

3 SLICES PINEAPPLE

2 OUNCES GIN

½ OUNCE SWEET VERMOUTH

½ OUNCE GRENADINE

ICE CUBES

Muddle the fruit in a shaker; then add the remaining ingredients. Shake with ice and strain into a chilled cocktail glass. Festoon with an additional slice each of orange and pineapple, and drink it in a blindingly sunny room filled with daisies and rainbows.

Serves 1

POOP-POOP-A-DOOP

Cocktail

While it might seem that this cocktail was created by new parents overwhelmed by the travails of diaper changes, it was actually a glamourous concoction popular among the 1930s *bon ton*. For example, the Poop-Poop-a-Doop was featured in a delightful 1933 book called *Hollywood Cocktails: Over 200 Excellent Recipes*, which sported the following subtitle:

> *Hollywood's Favorite Cocktail Book,*
> *Including a Cocktail Served at Each of the*
> *Smartest Stars' Rendevous*
> *(Whenever It Becomes Legal to Serve)*

The cocktail's name evoked the flapperish cry immortalized by Jazz Age cartoon Betty Boop; the internationally famous exclamation even served as a movie title (*Boop-Oop-A-Doop*, 1932), in which the curvaceous Miss Boop stars as a circus lion tamer and fights off the lecherous ringmaster.

½ OUNCE RUM

½ OUNCE DRY GIN

½ OUNCE SWEDISH PUNSCH

1 DASH APRICOT BRANDY

ICE CUBES

Shake with ice, strain into a chilled cocktail glass,
and sprinkle with coquettish glances.

Serves 1

"Martinis are like a woman's breasts: one is not enough.
Two: perfect, and three is too many."

Old saying

POOR DEAR OLD THING

Cocktail

❄ FOR WHEN YOU'RE FEELING NEGLECTED & UNPOPULAR ❄

This old-fashioned cocktail is your new go-to consolation when the phone has stopped ringing, invitations have stopped coming in, you've been given a Siberia table in your favorite restaurant, and not even your kisses-for-everyone Golden Retriever looks up when you come into the room.

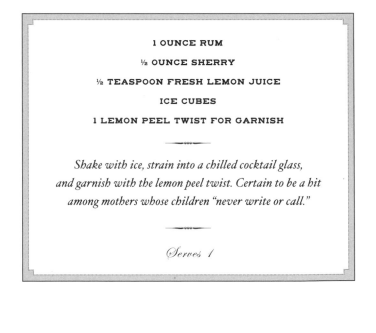

1 OUNCE RUM

½ OUNCE SHERRY

½ TEASPOON FRESH LEMON JUICE

ICE CUBES

1 LEMON PEEL TWIST FOR GARNISH

———

Shake with ice, strain into a chilled cocktail glass, and garnish with the lemon peel twist. Certain to be a hit among mothers whose children "never write or call."

———

Serves 1

POUSSE L'AMOUR

Fancy Drink

❊ AN IMBIBABLE WORK OF ART ❊

Another member of the pousse-café family, in which each
ingredient is added from densest to the least dense to achieve
the layered effect (see also the Parisien Cocktail, page 131, and
the Symphony of Moist Joy Fancy Drink, page 182).

Serve this eighteenth-century French libation to a fashion-
and décor-minded group; fans of Piet Mondrian will especially
appreciate the painstakingly achieved color-blocking of the drink.

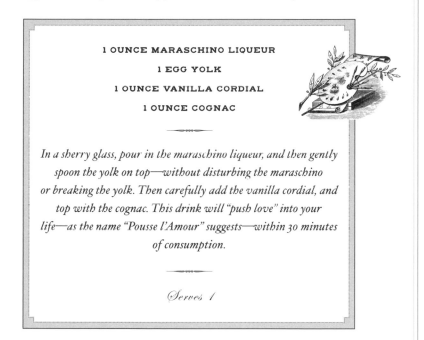

1 OUNCE MARASCHINO LIQUEUR

1 EGG YOLK

1 OUNCE VANILLA CORDIAL

1 OUNCE COGNAC

*In a sherry glass, pour in the maraschino liqueur, and then gently
spoon the yolk on top—without disturbing the maraschino
or breaking the yolk. Then carefully add the vanilla cordial, and
top with the cognac. This drink will "push love" into your
life—as the name "Pousse l'Amour" suggests—within 30 minutes
of consumption.*

Serves 1

THE DAISY

A tall potation made of liquor, lime or lemon juice, and grenadine—which is occasionally replaced by a cordial or liqueur. Think of it as a Shirley Temple for chic adults.

A delicious Daisy standard:

....

RUM DAISY

2 ounces light rum
½ ounce grenadine
1 ounce fresh lime juice
½ teaspoon sugar
Ice cubes

Shake with ice and pour into an ice-filled tumbler. Can be adorned with fruits and berries.

SERVES 1

....

PRAIRIE CHICKEN
— Cocktail —

It's hard to imagine Ma or Pa Ingalls sipping cocktails out on the Kansas plains—but perhaps their live-wire, high-living, dancing-and-singing neighbor Mr. Edwards would have appreciated this pre–Prohibition era beverage. That is, if he ever made it out east to the refined bar of New York City's Waldorf-Astoria, where the Prairie Chicken was served:

1 OUNCE GIN

1 EGG

SALT

PEPPER

Slide the yolk, unbroken, into a red wine glass, and cover it with the gin. Sprinkle with a bit of salt and pepper. Best enjoyed at dawn, when it will help you recover from a night of fiddling under the harvest moon, and fortify you for a day of log-cabin building.

Serves 1

PRAIRIE OYSTER

Cocktail

Bestowed upon the world by the Savoy, the Prairie Oyster was treated for years as the ultimate hangover cure. Like the Martini in the sixties and the Cosmopolitan in the nineties, the Prairie Oyster accrued a certain cultural currency, and always seemed to end up in the clutches of glamorously decadent literary and cinematic characters. James Bond confessed in *Thunderball* that his breakfast often consisted of "a couple of aspirins and a prairie oyster." Sally Bowles—the scandalous heroine of the famous film *Cabaret* and the book *Goodbye to Berlin*—downs them left and right:

> "'Would you like a Prairie Oyster?' [Sally] produced glasses, eggs and a bottle of Worchester sauce from the boot cupboard under the dismantled washstand: 'I practically live on them.' Dexterously, she broke the eggs into the glasses, added the sauce, and stirred up the mixture with the end of a fountain pen: 'They're about all I can afford.' She was back on the sofa again, daintily curled up."

As one journalist once wrote of the cocktail, "it will either restore you—or finish you off." Either way, you'll be relieved of the hangover.

1 EGG YOLK, UNBROKEN

2 DASHES VINEGAR

1 TEASPOON WORCESTERSHIRE SAUCE

1 TEASPOON KETCHUP

BLACK PEPPER

———

Gently slide the egg yolk into a highball glass.
Pour the Worcestershire sauce, vinegar, and ketchup over the yolk;
add one dash of black pepper. Some recipes also call for a dash
of celery salt. Bravely gulp it down without breaking the yolk.
Use any leftovers to spackle cracks of your driveway.

———

Serves 1

"White 'ere red, steady head
Red 'ere white, one hell of a night."

OLD SAYING ABOUT THE CORRECT DRINKING SEQUENCE OF WINE

RED SNAPPER

Cocktail

Historians of the bar have long bickered about the origins of the Bloody Mary. While the name of the first genius to combine tomato juice and vodka remains unclear, the St. Regis Hotel of New York City certainly played a role in popularizing the drink—albeit under a different moniker. In 1934, St. Regis bartender Fernand Petiot was asked by a prominent Russian patron to replicate a certain vodka cocktail he had sampled in Paris. Petiot obliged, adding his own combination of salt, pepper, lemon, and Worcestershire sauce. Dubbed the "Red Snapper," it remains a patron saint cocktail of the St. Regis today.

The original 1934 recipe:

1 OUNCE VODKA

2 OUNCES TOMATO JUICE

1 DASH FRESH LEMON JUICE

2 DASHES SALT

2 DASHES BLACK PEPPER

2 DASHES CAYENNE PEPPER

3 DASHES WORCESTERSHIRE SAUCE

ICE CUBES

1 CELERY STALK FOR GARNISH

Mix and serve in a tall Collins glass filled with ice.
Garnish with the celery stalk and a placard proclaiming,
"I am Not a Bloody Mary."

Serves 1

THE GRIEVING WIFE

HISTORICAL ALCOHOLIC ODES
TO THE BEREAVED FEMALE

In the popular imagination of yesterday's bartenders, widows had a grand old time. In drinks commemorating them, these ladies dreamed soulfully, kissed sweetly, and generally made merry.

. . . —————— . . .

THE MERRY WIDOW COCKTAIL
(one variation)

½ ounce French vermouth
½ ounce Dubonnet
Ice cubes

Stir with ice and strain into a chilled cocktail glass.

THE WIDOW'S KISS COCKTAIL

1 ounce Calvados
½ ounce yellow Chartreuse
½ ounce Benedictine
1 dash Angostura bitters
Ice cubes

Stir with ice and strain into a chilled cocktail glass.

THE WIDOW'S DREAM COCKTAIL

1 ounce Benedictine
1 egg
Ice cubes
Cream

Shake the Benedectine and egg with ice and strain into a lowball glass. Float a little bit of cream on the top.

EACH SERVES 1

REFORM

Cocktail

❄ **TO HELP YOU MEND YOUR SORRY WAYS** ❄

This drink is especially handy just after the New Year, when you are attempting to uphold a lengthy list of ambitious resolutions. The old-fashioned Reform Cocktail helps build that precious resolve to lose weight, learn French, save more money, write more often to Mother, and other admirable pipe dreams.

---

1 OUNCE SHERRY

1 OUNCE FRENCH VERMOUTH

2 DASHES ANGOSTURA BITTERS

ICE CUBES

1 ORANGE PEEL FOR GARNISH

Shake with ice and strain into a chilled cocktail glass.
Garnish with the orange peel, a twist of self-reproach,
and a teaspoon of self-discipline.

Serves 1

RHETT BUTLER
Cocktail

❋ FOR WHEN YOU FRANKLY DON'T GIVE A DAMN ❋

Serve this cocktail to a cocksure, suave, independent gentleman in your life—or sip it to shore up your own measure of irreverence. While you're imbibing, take a moment to recall that Rhett's famous give-a-damn line is nothing compared to one of his other gems:

"With enough courage, you can do without a reputation."

1½ OUNCES SOUTHERN COMFORT BOURBON

¼ OUNCE CURAÇAO

½ OUNCE FRESH LIME JUICE

½ OUNCE FRESH LEMON JUICE

½ TEASPOON SUGAR

SHAVED ICE

Mix and pour into a Champagne glass filled with shaved ice. Serve alongside the

SCARLETT O'HARA COCKTAIL:

1½ OUNCES SOUTHERN COMFORT BOURBON

1 OUNCE CRANBERRY JUICE

1 DASH FRESH LIME JUICE

ICE CUBES

Shake with ice and strain through a green velvet curtain into a chilled cocktail glass.

Each Serves 1

ROBINSON CRUSOE
Cocktail

In this era of over-communication, over-connectedness, and over-sharing, who on earth *doesn't* occasionally want to get shipwrecked on an uncharted, un-peopled island? Although admittedly it would be nicer to shack up on a slightly less violent island than the one that hosted Robinson Crusoe himself in his eponymous 1719 novel; after all, he had to deal with surly cannibals, mutineers, and all sorts of other nuisances.

To simulate the castaway experience without the inconveniences, simply toss your handheld into the sea and mix yourself one of these transporting vintage concoctions.

1½ OUNCES RUM

1½ OUNCES PINEAPPLE JUICE

ICE CUBES

1 COCONUT SHELL

*Stir the rum and pineapple juice together with ice,
pour into the coconut shell, and serve.*

Serves 1

ROLLS-ROYCE

Cocktail

The Rolls—that status car driven by film stars, tycoons, and dictators for nearly a century—has long been such an emblem of luxury that it's used as a standard against which other luxuries are measured, as in, "So-and-so is the Rolls-Royce of Champagnes" or "XYZ is the Rolls-Royce of pens."

Even if your budget is more Mazda than Rolls, the latter's namesake cocktail will leave you feeling like a million bucks.

---

1 OUNCE GIN

½ OUNCE FRENCH VERMOUTH

½ OUNCE ITALIAN VERMOUTH

1 DASH BENEDICTINE

ICE CUBES

---

*Stir with ice and strain into a chilled cocktail glass.
The hand with which you grip this glass should be absolutely
heaving with rocks—whether real or aspirational.*

Serves 1

GUNPOWDER AND CASHEW NUTS

BISCUITS

All sorts of nineteenth-century concoctions call for the inclusion of biscuits and bread in their preparations. *The Family Receipt Book* (1819), for example, includes a drink recipe called "Drink for the Summer." Into a vat of sherry, "cyder," "perry," and brandy, one was instructed to "toast a biscuit very brown and throw it hot into the liquor."

CASHEW NUTS

These were used in an alcoholic drink called "Balm of Mankind," along with Peruvian balsam and dried heads of wormwood, according to *The Art of Confectionary* (1866).

OATMEAL

It was plunked into a drink called "White Caudle" in a recipe from *Practical Housewife* (1860).

POWDERED FLORENCE IRIS

Rather difficult to find today, this ingredient was used in an "Anisette" recipe in *The Art of Confectionary* (1866). Another anisette calls for musk-seed and pearl gunpowder tea.

SCURVY-GRASS

Also known as "spoonwort," this roughage was used to make "Scurvy-Grass Wine" in a recipe from *Mackenzie's 5000 Recipes* (1829).

SEAWATER

This was an ingredient in an ancient Roman wine mixture, along with pine resin.

TOPS OF FIR

Ambitious homemakers would add these to a potion of "wheaten malt," oatmeal, ground beans, and "ten new laid eggs," with the aim of producing "German Liquor Mum."

[PLATE XI]

Runt's Ambition Cocktail

RUNT'S AMBITION
Cocktail

❋   TO SERVE TO MEN WITH NAPOLEON COMPLEX   ❋

Although he was the average height of a man of his era (various accounts place the exact measurement between 5'2" and 5'7"), French Emperor Napoleon Bonaparte has gone down in history as a rather squat individual. The affliction known as "Napoleon Complex" is generally said to be endured by certain short men tortured about their height (or lack thereof), who in turn over-compensate in other aspects of their lives.

Serving an ambitious runt this vintage concoction could have either one of two effects:

> 1 / It might take the edge off for the evening and help him forget his woes,

or,

> 2 / It might give him courage to invade a vulnerable country.

CONTINUED ON NEXT PAGE ⟫→

2 OUNCES RUM

2 OUNCES GIN

2 OUNCES WHISKEY

2 OUNCES PORT WINE

ICE CUBES

———

Shake with ice and strain into a chilled cocktail glass.
Can also be served in a chilled Champagne coupe glass,
the shape of which is sometimes said to have been inspired
by the breast of Empress Josephine, Napoleon's wife.

———

Serves 2

"I drink Champagne when I win, to celebrate . . .
and I drink Champagne when I lose, to console myself."

Napoleon Bonaparte

THREE HUNDRED YEARS OF DRUNKENNESS

○○○ AMERICA'S OLDEST BAR ○○○

This honorific is usually bestowed upon Laffite's Blacksmith Shop Bar, located on the corner of Bourbon and St. Philip Streets in New Orleans. It is alternatively cited as the oldest structure used as a bar in the United States, the oldest continually occupied bar, and the oldest building in the French Quarter.

Built between 1722 and 1732, the building somehow survived two near-disastrous fires and was allegedly used by two pirate brothers extraordinaire—Jean and Pierre Lafitte—as a base (or a "blind") for their smuggling operations in the late eighteenth century. There were, of course, related rumors that the Laffites had buried riches in the yards surrounding the shop, prompting generations of treasure-hunters to scavenge the area.

Some claim that Jean Laffite has never left the bar: Reported sightings of his ghost are frequent. Occasionally his apparition is spotted twirling his moustache in the dark corners of the first floor; at other times, he is seen hanging from the rafters. According to one local historian of the paranormal, "The privateer's frequent appearance in the women's restroom suggests that Laffite's interest in the ladies has not diminished over the years."

Writers Tennessee Williams and Lucius Beebe frequented Laffite's and reportedly drank on the house. At night, the bar is still lit only by candlelight, and its past never feels far away.

Salomé

Cocktail

One of history's more storied seductresses, Salomé first turned up in the Bible and has inspired countless works of art ever since. Here she is mentioned in the Gospel of Matthew:

> "[O]n Herod's birthday, the daughter of Herodias danced
> before them: and pleased Herod. Whereupon he promised with
> an oath, to give her whatsoever she would ask of him. But she
> being instructed before by her mother, said: Give me here in
> a dish the head of John the Baptist. And the king was struck
> sad: yet because of his oath, and for them that sat with him at
> table, he commanded it to be given. And he sent, and beheaded
> John in the prison."

Playwright Oscar Wilde (see Dandy Cocktail, page 54) later put his own psychological twist on the scenario: In his play *Salomé* (1891), the title character takes a carnal interest in John the Baptist, who spurns her affections. She then very reasonably demands that he be executed. At the play's conclusion, the triumphant Salomé holds up John's severed head and kisses it.

Her namesake cocktail—once served at many of the early twentieth century's great bars and hotels—is perfect for those who wish to tap into their hidden wells of dangerous eroticism.

½ OUNCE DRY GIN

½ OUNCE FRENCH VERMOUTH

½ OUNCE DUBONNET

ICE CUBES

Shake with ice and strain through seven veils into a platter.

Serves 1

"Wine was created for the solace of man, as a slight compensation, we are told, for the creation of woman."

The Savoy Cocktail Book • 1930

THE FLIP

You don't see Flips around much anymore, but they should hasten back to bar menus, *tout de suite*. Usually made with one egg, one teaspoon of sugar, and two ounces of liquor, they "combine the curative properties of an Egg Nog and a Fizz, are good early-morning or bedtime drinks, and considered good builder-uppers," asserts legendary bartender Trader Vic in his 1947 *Bartender's Guide*.

What follows: a couple of old-fashioned flips that would likely appeal to modern palates.

CHAMPAGNE FLIP

2 ounces Champagne
½ teaspoon simple syrup
1 egg yolk
Ice cubes

Shake with ice and strain into a chilled Champagne coupe glass. Trader Vic recommends that you also "add a dash of brandy."

CHOCOLATE FLIP

1 ounce yellow Chartreuse
1 ounce maraschino liqueur
1 teaspoon cocoa powder
1 teaspoon powdered sugar
1 egg
Ice cubes

Shake with ice and strain into a chilled wine goblet.

EACH SERVES 1

SATAN'S WHISKERS

Cocktail

❄ FOR WHEN YOU'RE FEELING DEVILISH ❄

Bartenders of bygone eras have conjured up the Devil with a plethora of cocktails: the Satan Cocktail, the Devil Cocktail, the Diablo, Devil's Leap, and so on (see "Saints and Sinners: Bygone Cocktails with Religious Undertones," page 110). They have even commemorated Satan's various body parts (the Devil's Tail, Devil's Fingers, etc.), but few are more spirited than the cocktails named for the Devil's *whiskers*.

Amusingly, you can order these whiskers "straight" or "curled":

FOR STRAIGHT SATANIC WHISKERS

½ OUNCE DRY GIN

½ OUNCE ITALIAN VERMOUTH

½ OUNCE FRENCH VERMOUTH

½ OUNCE FRESH ORANGE JUICE

¼ OUNCE GRAND MARNIER

¼ OUNCE ORANGE BITTERS

ICE CUBES

Shake with ice and strain into a large chilled cocktail glass.

FOR CURLED SATANIC WHISKERS

Simply swap in orange curaçao for the Grand Marnier.

Each serves 1

SCHNORKEL

Cocktail

❄ TO GO DEEP-SEA DIVING—WITHOUT THE OCEAN ❄

Not to be confused with the "Schnozzle cocktail," this old-fangled drink—reportedly named after a historical submarine—will send you straight to the lagoon, figuratively speaking. Perfect for times when you are hankering after a maritime vacation, but are too short on funds.

2 OUNCES RUM

½ OUNCE PERNOD

1 OUNCE FRESH LIME JUICE

1 TEASPOON SUGAR

ICE CUBES

Shake with ice and strain into a highball glass.
Best accessorized with a scuba suit.

Serves 1

HAIR OF THE DOG

SOCIALLY ACCEPTABLE
MORNING COCKTAILS

According to conventions of yore, the practice of morning drinking hasn't always been a sure-fire sign that you should be sliding down the banister straight into an AA meeting.

"The mid-morning slug" might seem like "an eminently unchristian practice," wrote Lucius Beebe in his seminal bartending bible, *The Stork Club Bar Book* (1946), but in the nineteenth century, "mid-morning was the first well-established cocktail hour."

"Hardy souls had a slug of rock and rye while shaving," he continued, "and [they] brushed their teeth in a light Moselle."

For Beebe, acceptable "restoratives" and "pick-me-ups" included the Manhattan, the dry Martini, Milk Punch, the Sherry Flip, and a bawdy beverage called the Rosalind Russell.

But the "most heroic of remedies," he contended, was the London Fog cocktail.

 LONDON FOG COCKTAIL

1½ ounces gin
½ ounce Pernod
Shaved ice

Frappé gin and Pernod with shaved ice and "serve while still frothing."

SERVES I

SCOFFLAW

Cocktail

❄   FOR WHEN YOU'RE FEELING REBELLIOUS   ❄

Here is an old-fashioned word that absolutely *must* stage a comeback: "Scofflaw" means "a person who flouts rules, conventions, or accepted practices." Downing the word's namesake cocktail will immediately give you courage to:

1 / Wear white after Labor Day

2 / Eat dessert before supper

3 / Don a red dress to a wedding

4 / Order a small, medium, or large coffee at Starbucks instead of a "tall," "grande," or "venti"

5 / Sprinkle Parmesan cheese on seafood pasta

. . . and all sorts of comparable acts of insurrection.

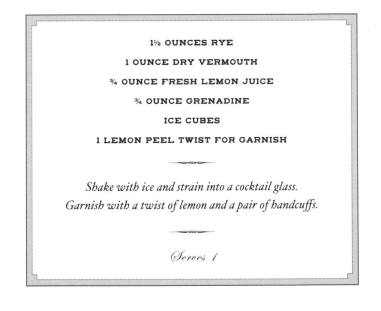

1½ OUNCES RYE

1 OUNCE DRY VERMOUTH

¾ OUNCE FRESH LEMON JUICE

¾ OUNCE GRENADINE

ICE CUBES

1 LEMON PEEL TWIST FOR GARNISH

Shake with ice and strain into a cocktail glass.
Garnish with a twist of lemon and a pair of handcuffs.

Serves 1

SHEIK'S BREATH

Cocktail

❋ TO CONJURE UP A ROMANTIC ARABIAN ADVENTURE ❋

Of course, it would help matters considerably if the sheik in question looked like Omar Sharif in his *Lawrence of Arabia* garb.

The recipe below—fished out of the depths of Trader Vic's 1947 *Bartender's Guide*—calls for the use of an ingredient called "caloric," also known as Swedish punsch. So make sure to pick some up next time you skip through Stockholm.

½ OUNCE GIN

½ OUNCE CALORIC

½ OUNCE FRESH LEMON JUICE

ICE CUBES

———

Shake with ice and strain into a chilled cocktail glass.
Best enjoyed while reclining in the Bedouin tents
of the Jordanian desert.

———

Serves 1

THE SHRUB

A concoction composed of brandy or rum, stewed fruits, and sugar; these ingredients were brewed together, aged in a sealed container, and then usually bottled. They were served hot in the winter and cold in the summer. The following 1829 recipe for Currant Shrub appeared in *MacKenzie's 5000 Receipts*:

> "Take white currants, when quite ripe, pick them off the stalks, and bruise them; strain out the juice through a cloth, and to two quarts of the juice put 2 lbs. of loaf sugar; when it is dissolved add to it a gallon of rum, then strain it through a flannel bag that will keep in the jelly, and it will run off clear; then bottle it for use."

If this is all too nineteenth century for you, try this more manageable, modernized version:

....

CURRANT SHRUB

8 cups currant juice
1½ pounds sugar
Brandy

Mix the currant juice and sugar in a large saucepan; boil it for ten minutes. Let the mixture cool, and for every two pints of sweetened juice, stir in 2 ounces of brandy. Bottle.

....

To serve shrub hot, pour two ounces of shrub mixture into a mug and top with boiling water. To serve it cold, pour two ounces of shrub into a tumbler or highball glass; add a few ice cubes and top off with seltzer.

SMART ALEC

Punch

❋ TO SERVE TO KNOW-IT-ALLS ❋

The phrase "Smart Alec" (meaning "an obnoxiously conceited and self-assertive person with pretensions to smartness or cleverness") makes a quaint alternative to its contemporary version, i.e., the comparatively crude "smart ass."

Other equally endearing, old-fashioned synonyms include:

Clever-clogs	Smarty pants
Clever Dick	Wiseacre
Smart nose	Wise guy

For eons, bartenders have had to contend with people of these descriptions, so it's hardly surprising that the phrase *Smart Alec* ended up commemorating a libation. Serve it to the "swellheads" in your life.

¾ OUNCE COGNAC

½ OUNCE COINTREAU

½ OUNCE YELLOW CHARTREUSE

1 DASH ORANGE BITTERS

ICE CUBES

Shake with ice, strain into a chilled cocktail glass, and garnish with a pair of smarty pants.

Serves 1

SOVIET
Cocktail

❄ TO HELP YOU FORMULATE A FIVE-YEAR PLAN ❄

When the future feels entirely too up-in-the-air and you become determined to impose a little structure, this drink will help you map it all out.

Another nifty attribute of the Soviet Cocktail: It has proven helpful in providing a release to those whose lives are feeling entirely too bureaucratic.

---

1 OUNCE VODKA

¾ OUNCE SHERRY

¾ OUNCE FRENCH VERMOUTH

ICE CUBES

Shake with ice, strain into a chilled cocktail glass,
and drink among comrades.

Serves 1

SPLITTING HEADACHE

Punch

This drink hails from the early nineteenth century, when headache remedies were likely limited to lying in dark rooms on fainting couches, with lace draped over one's eyes. While it's unclear whether the Splitting Headache Punch was considered curative or causal, we can surmise that it would have offered headache sufferers at least a brief respite from their ailments.

Happily, the recipe below makes enough to treat a whole village:

½ CUP RUM

½ DOZEN CRUSHED CLOVES

A PINCH EACH CINNAMON, GINGER, AND NUTMEG

½ TEASPOON FRESH LIME JUICE

2 QUARTS (8 CUPS) BOTTLED ALE

Mix the rum, cloves, and spices together and strain into a punch bowl; add the lime juice and bottled ale.

Dunk your whole head into the bowl to experience the full medicinal effect.

Serves 10-12

STOLEN KISSES
Cocktail

❊ FOR WHEN YOU'RE FEELING SURREPTITIOUS ❊

One of the great joys in life: stealing a kiss from a forbidden lover. The original version of this cocktail was composed of nothing less than the distilled essence of every romantic stolen kiss since the beginning of time. Since that recipe proved impossible to replicate in any great quantity, a gifted bartender formulated the following approximation:

¾ OUNCE PERNOD

¾ OUNCE GIN

½ EGG WHITE

½ TEASPOON SIMPLE SYRUP

ICE CUBES

Shake with ice and strain into a chilled cocktail glass.
Female imbibers should reapply lipstick after each sip
so as not to look suspicious.

Serves 1

A CERTAIN UNCONFIRMABLE RUMOR ABOUT THE EVOLUTION OF THE MARTINI

The following assertion comes courtesy of a former bartender at the once-legendary Cedar Tavern in New York City (see "Bars of the Modern Art Movements," page 194).

The reason that so many people have forsaken gin Martinis for vodka Martinis over the years: Disapproving bosses and clients back at the office can smell gin on one's breath after a three-Martini lunch, but the odor of vodka cannot be detected.

Is this the true cause behind the vodka Martini's rise in popularity? Perhaps. Evidence of sensible strategizing? Absolutely.

SWAN SONG
Cocktail

❊   TO MAKE YOUR EXIT MEMORABLE   ❊

The official definition of a swan song: "The last act, appearance, performance, or utterance of a person before retirement or death." According to an old European myth, swans sing as they die; not just any old tune, but a wrenching, captivating song.

The bottom line: We all have to go sometime; one might as well make a memorable last impression. What follows is a short list of deathbed swan-song lines allegedly uttered by luminaries over the centuries:

"Et tu, brute?" • JULIUS CAESAR

"Either those curtains go, or I do." • OSCAR WILDE

"I never should have switched from Scotch to martinis." • HUMPHREY BOGART

"Friends applaud; the comedy is finished." • LUDWIG VAN BEETHOVEN

"I'm bored with it all." • WINSTON CHURCHILL

"Good night, my darlings. I'll see you tomorrow." • NOËL COWARD

"I must go in; the fog is rising." • EMILY DICKINSON

"Why not? Yeah." • TIMOTHY LEARY

"God bless . . . God damn." • JAMES THURBER

"Last words are for fools who haven't said enough." • KARL MARX

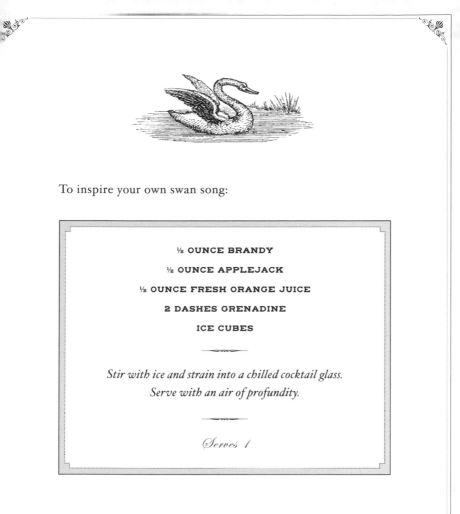

To inspire your own swan song:

½ OUNCE BRANDY

½ OUNCE APPLEJACK

½ OUNCE FRESH ORANGE JUICE

2 DASHES GRENADINE

ICE CUBES

———

Stir with ice and strain into a chilled cocktail glass.
Serve with an air of profundity.

———

Serves 1

"To drink a glass of sherry when you can get a dry martini is like
taking a stagecoach when you can travel by the Orient Express."

ATTRIBUTED TO *W. Somerset Maugham* • AUTHOR

THE RATAFIA

A homemade mainstay in 19th century America and a centuries-old specialty in Italy and France, the Ratafia was a sweet cordial made from wine, brandy, or another spirit, and flavored with fruit, almonds, seeds, or fruit kernels. A fairly typical Ratafia recipe comes to us courtesy of *The Art of Confectionary* (1866):

JUNIPER-BERRY RATAFIA

"Take eight ounces of juniper berries, one drachm of cinnamon, two drachms of coriander, and half a drachm of mace; bruise the whole, and steep them for fifteen days in fourteen pints of brandy; squeeze through a cloth, and add a syrup made with seven pounds of sugar, and filter."

A modern champion of the Ratafia was culinary writer Jane Grigson, who wrote beautifully about them in her now-classic cookbook, *Good Things* (originally published in 1971). Consult it to acquaint yourself with how to make delectable Quince Ratafia and a splendid Ratafia of Red Fruits. A warning: they are only to be attempted by the patient at heart: Grigson advised that Ratafias only reach their mellowest and most subtle after "a month or two or three."

SWEET PATOOTIE

Cocktail

❄ TO EXPRESS NOURISHING AFFECTION ❄

This phrase is 1920s slang for "sweetheart" or "pretty girl."
Word historians believe that it perhaps stemmed from
a corruption of the word "potato." If true, the so-called
corruption was an improvement: Ladies likely far preferred
being kissed and squeezed and called a "sweet patootie"
than referred to as a lumpen potato.

---

1 OUNCE GIN

½ OUNCE COINTREAU

½ OUNCE FRESH ORANGE JUICE

ICE CUBES

Shake with ice and strain into a heart-shaped candy box.

Serves 1

SYMPHONY OF MOIST JOY

Fancy Drink

❄ LIQUID BEETHOVEN ❄

One of the more curiously named old-guard cocktails out there. Whether you attribute cultivated or lewd connotations to it is your prerogative. If your inclination is the former, serve this drink at an at-home concert or musical evening. But take care not to invite too many people, for the Symphony of Moist Joy is damn hard to make; after all, it's yet another member of the pousse-café family, in which each ingredient is added from densest to the least dense to achieve the layered effect (see also the Parisien Cocktail, page 131, and the Pousse l'Amour Fancy Drink, page 147).

½ OUNCE GRENADINE

½ OUNCE YELLOW CHARTREUSE

½ OUNCE CRÈME DE MENTHE

½ OUNCE COGNAC

*Pour ingredients carefully into a chilled pousse-café glass
in the order listed, making sure that they don't mix.
Festoon with cherries, eighth notes, and a twisted violin string.*

Serves 1

TAKE IT OR LEAVE IT
Cocktail

❄ TO SERVE WHEN MAKING ULTIMATUMS ❄

Clearly this cocktail shows that you mean business. Carry a thermos of it for ultimatums made on the run. The apricot brandy and grenadine provide *just* enough sugar to sweeten the deal.

1 OUNCE DRY GIN

½ OUNCE APRICOT BRANDY

½ OUNCE FRENCH VERMOUTH

1 DASH FRESH LEMON JUICE

1 DASH GRENADINE

ICE CUBES

Shake with ice and strain into a chilled cocktail glass. Make sure to slam the glass down on the bar emphatically when finished.

Serves 1

T.N.T.

Cocktail

❉ FOR WHEN YOU'RE FEELING DESTRUCTIVE ❉

Also handy when you feel the need to start something from scratch: your relationship, your job, your house, your whole *life*. Blow it up and begin anew. This drink will give you the *cojones* to do so.

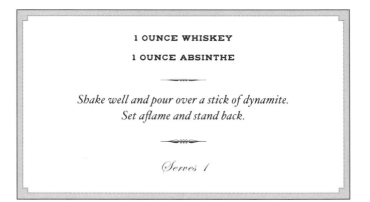

1 OUNCE WHISKEY

1 OUNCE ABSINTHE

Shake well and pour over a stick of dynamite.
Set aflame and stand back.

Serves 1

[PLATE XII]

T.N.T. Cocktail

THE GREEN CURE-ALL

UNLIKELY USES FOR ABSINTHE OVER THE CENTURIES

An extremely strong, anise-flavored alcoholic drink, absinthe derives its famous particularity from the flowers and leaves of the bitter herb *Artemisia absinthium* (i.e., wormwood). So popular in nineteenth-century France that the time between 5 p.m. and 7 p.m. became known as "l'heure verte" (the Green Hour), absinthe also made its way to American shores and was particularly exalted in New Orleans by a chicly degenerate creative class.

Usually bright green (earning it the moniker *La Fée Verte*, or "The Green Fairy"), this drink also contained trace elements of the chemical thujone, whose occasionally hallucinogenic effects gave absinthe a reputation for causing madness; the beverage was slapped with a nearly century-long ban in much of the Western world that lasted until the 1990s.

It is ironic, then, that before it became a recreational libation, absinthe was considered a cure-all for many different ailments, ranging from indigestion to hubris:

••• In ancient Greece, wormwood leaves soaked in wine or spirits were reportedly prescribed as a cure for rheumatism, jaundice, and anemia.

••• Ancient Romans used it to smite out bad breath—and as an elixir of youth.

••• According to one source, an ancient Roman custom at the end of chariot races involved having the champion drink a cup of wormwood leaves soaked in wine "to remind him that even glory has its bitter side."

••• In the early 1800s, absinthe was prescribed to French troops in North Africa and Indochina to fight off malaria and dysentery; its apparent success in this regard imbued the drink with patriotic connotations. (Another absinthe irony: A century later, the drink would be blamed for French defeats during World War I and stripped of its halo.)

"She is a Martinique aristocrat who lives in Fort de France but also has an apartment in Paris. We are sitting on the terrace of her house, an airy, elegant house that looks as if it was made of wooden lace: it reminds me of certain old New Orleans houses. We are drinking iced mint tea slightly flavored with absinthe, [which] she pours from a dazzling emerald green decanter."

Truman Capote • MUSIC FOR CHAMELEONS

TOP HAT

Cocktail

❄ **TO HONOR THE LEGENDARY FRED ASTAIRE** ❄

When tasked with describing Astaire (1899–1987), screen siren Marlene Dietrich came up with the following three words:

"Elegant! Elegant! Elegant!"

Some actors become forever associated with specific items of clothing, and for dancer and film star Fred Astaire, that wardrobe item was the top hat. Both garment and wearer epitomized Old Hollywood at its most suave and glamorous. Astaire starred in a now legendary 1935 film called *Top Hat*, which featured timeless classic tunes "Cheek to Cheek" and "Top Hat, White Tie, and Tails." Sip this cocktail while watching his whole roster of films and reveling in his inimitable sophistication and wit.

"T'was a woman who drove me to drink.
I never had the courtesy to thank her."

W. C. Fields • COMEDIAN, ACTOR, AND WRITER

2 SLICES PINEAPPLE

1 SLICE LEMON

1 SLICE ORANGE

1½ TEASPOONS GRENADINE

1½ OUNCES RUM

SHAVED ICE

———

*Muddle the fruit and the grenadine. Add the rum
and shaved ice, and then shake well. Strain into a large
chilled cocktail glass. Be sure to serve it alongside a*

GINGER ROGERS COCKTAIL:

½ OUNCE GIN

½ OUNCE APRICOT BRANDY

½ OUNCE FRENCH VERMOUTH

1 TEASPOON FRESH LEMON JUICE

ICE CUBES

1 MARASCHINO CHERRY FOR GARNISH

———

*Shake with ice and strain into a chilled cocktail glass.
Garnish with a maraschino cherry and a satin dancing slipper.*

———

Each Serves 1

UP-TO-DATE

Cocktail

❋ TO DRAG YOU OUT OF THE DARK AGES ❋

It doesn't matter how hopelessly last-season your wardrobe is, or that your idea of contemporary fiction is Edith Wharton. Upon sipping this concoction, you will instantly be transformed into a savvy trendsetter, abreast of the latest vogues. Tried-and-true, the Up-to-Date has been rendering its drinkers *au courant* since the World War I era.

Keep the recipe a secret, however—true tastemakers must remain ahead of the pack, not a part of it.

---

1 OUNCE RYE OR BOURBON

1 OUNCE SHERRY

2 DASHES GRAND MARNIER

2 DASHES ANGOSTURA BITTERS

ICE CUBES

———

Shake with ice and strain into a chilled cocktail glass.
Serve with a superior, knowing, envy-inspiring smile.

———

Serves 1

VERITAS

Cocktail

❅ FOR WHEN YOU NEED A STRAIGHT ANSWER ❅

Veritas means "truth" in Latin, so administer this vintage cocktail right away when someone is beating around the bush.

A short list of ideal Veritas Cocktail recipients:

1 / Witnesses under cross-examination

2 / Suspect lovers who are being evasive about their last-night whereabouts

3 / Roommates who may or may not have consumed your Fruity Pebbles

4 / Spouses who may or may not have read your diary

5 / Landlords who are dodging the question about whether your rent will be raised next year

To create the truth serum:

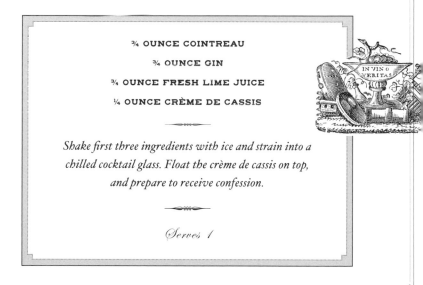

¾ OUNCE COINTREAU

¾ OUNCE GIN

¾ OUNCE FRESH LIME JUICE

¼ OUNCE CRÈME DE CASSIS

Shake first three ingredients with ice and strain into a chilled cocktail glass. Float the crème de cassis on top, and prepare to receive confession.

Serves 1

WELCOME STRANGER
Cocktail

❄ TO DEMONSTRATE HOSPITALITY ❄

The American South has long been concerned with pleasing strangers. One particularly lovely Southern hospitality ritual: leaving an empty space at the dinner table, in case a hungry, unexpected guest shows up. It's no wonder such an effort is made, either: Let us not forget the famous utterance of Blanche Dubois—an emblem of Southern womanhood—during her final scene of *A Streetcar Named Desire*:

> *"Whoever you are, I have always depended on the kindness of strangers."*

Her swan song reminds us that we might all end up one day at the mercy of strangers, so let's reinstate a little kindness toward one another—starting with the Welcome Stranger Cocktail. Have a vat of it waiting in the front foyer at all times, as sort of a karmic insurance.

"There comes a time in every woman's life when the only thing that helps is a glass of champagne."

Bette Davis • *OLD ACQUAINTANCE* (1943)

¼ OUNCE SWEDISH PUNSCH

¼ OUNCE BRANDY

¼ OUNCE GIN

¼ OUNCE GRENADINE

¼ OUNCE FRESH ORANGE JUICE

¼ OUNCE FRESH LEMON JUICE

ICE CUBES

———

Shake with ice and strain into a chilled cocktail glass.
Seat the cocktail at the table's place of honor,
and tuck it to sleep in a feather bed.

———

Serves 1

BARS OF THE
MODERN ART MOVEMENTS

For hundreds of years, certain bars, hotels, and restaurants have co-opted the auras of the famous artists who frequented the establishments. In Paris, the Dingo and La Closerie des Lilas became synonymous with Hemingway. In New York City, the Algonquin is now forever linked with Dorothy Parker and her vicious Round Table; the same goes for the Plaza Hotel and F. Scott Fitzgerald.

Following World War II, three Manhattan bars played particularly crucial roles as incubators, in which important subsequent art movements were created:

· · · ———∿∾⟋⟍∾⟋⟍∿——— · · ·

CEDAR TAVERN

A storied dump, the Cedar Tavern occupied several locations throughout its history, but its heyday took place at 24 University Place, where it became the 1950s hangout for a rowdy crowd of painters and writers, including Jackson Pollock, Willem de Kooning, Mark Rothko, Franz Kline, Allen Ginsberg, Jack Kerouac, Frank O'Hara, and LeRoi Jones.

The Tavern's most celebrated patron, Pollock, was reportedly banned after ripping the men's room door from its hinges; ditto for Kerouac, who allegedly peed in an ashtray. The neighborhood was dangerous, muggings were common, and the early allure of the Tavern appears to have been its cheap alcohol; still, historians consider it an important incubator of the now-iconic Abstract Expressionist movement.

MAX'S KANSAS CITY

"Max's Kansas City was the exact place where Pop Art and Pop Life came together," Pop Art icon Andy Warhol once said. A favorite haunt of Warhol and his entourage from the Factory during the 1960s and 70s, the nightclub—located at 213 Park Avenue South—also hosted artists Robert Rauschenberg, Larry Rivers, Patti Smith, Robert Mapplethorpe, and Roy Lichtenstein. The Velvet Underground, Iggy Pop, and David Bowie all played there, and Max's Kansas City became seen as the crucible of the rebellion art and punk rock of that era.

MAGOO'S

In the early 1980s, Tribeca was one of the last affordable Manhattan neighborhoods in which New York artists could set up camp. Real artists had decamped from SoHo years earlier, and Magoo's was one of the few artists' bars with real street credibility left; it became a crucible for the "Pictures Generation" of photographers, including the legendary Cindy Sherman. The bar's owner would reportedly settle tabs with art instead of currency.

WINCHELL

Cocktail

❊ FOR WHEN YOU'RE FEELING GOSSIPY ❊

Although officially described in biographies as a newspaper and radio commentator, Walter Winchell (1897–1972) began his journalism career as an old-fashioned, vituperative gossip columnist. He got his start in 1924 at the late tabloid *Evening Graphic*, and became quip-famous on the topic of his new profession ("Gossip is the art of saying nothing in a way that leaves practically nothing unsaid"; "The same thing happened today that happened yesterday, only to different people"; "Today's gossip is tomorrow's headline").

Winchell was said to be fond of the Pink Lady Cocktail (a concoction of apple brandy, dry gin, lemon juice, grenadine, and egg white), but a different mid-century cocktail with a more masculine roster of ingredients bore his name. Use it to get others plastered and tease out their deepest secrets:

1 OUNCE COGNAC

1 OUNCE DRY GIN

¼ OUNCE COINTREAU

¼ OUNCE FRESH LEMON JUICE

ICE CUBES

---

*Shake with ice, strain into a chilled cocktail glass,
and contrive to look trustworthy.*

Serves 1

X.Y.Z.
Cocktail

❄ TO SERVE TO ELEMENTARY SCHOOL TEACHERS ❄

This mid-century drink will certainly take the edge off tense parent-teacher conferences and diffuse tensions when served at PTA meetings. And—as a bottled teacher gift from junior—it makes an excellent alternative to the been-there-done-that red apple.

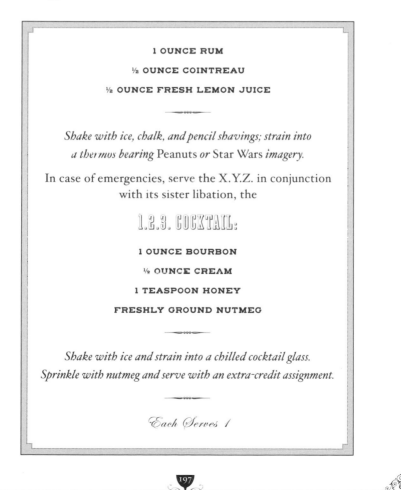

1 OUNCE RUM

½ OUNCE COINTREAU

½ OUNCE FRESH LEMON JUICE

Shake with ice, chalk, and pencil shavings; strain into a thermos bearing Peanuts *or* Star Wars *imagery.*

In case of emergencies, serve the X.Y.Z. in conjunction with its sister libation, the

1.2.3. COCKTAIL:

1 OUNCE BOURBON

½ OUNCE CREAM

1 TEASPOON HONEY

FRESHLY GROUND NUTMEG

Shake with ice and strain into a chilled cocktail glass. Sprinkle with nutmeg and serve with an extra-credit assignment.

Each Serves 1

HEAR ME ROAR

OLD-GUARD COCKTAILS NAMED
AFTER ANIMALS

Depending on the dispenser and the drinker, booze can float like a butterfly or sting like a bee. It comes as no surprise, then, that so many historical cocktails reference creatures of the Amazon, the barnyard, and all of the feral places in between.

Alligator Cocktail

Baby Kitty Cocktail

Barking Dog Cocktail

Bee's Knees Cocktail / *pg. 29*

Big Bad Wolf Cocktail / *pg. 32*

Bloodhound Cocktail / *pg. 35*

Boa Constrictor Cocktail

Bulldog Cocktail

Cat's Eye Cocktail

Caterpillar Cocktail

Crow Cocktail

Dog's Nose Cocktail

Eagle's Dream Cocktail

Elephant's Ear Cocktail

Elephant's Milk Cocktail

Elk Cocktail

Flying Fish Cocktail

Goat's Delight Cocktail / *pg. 74*

Grasshopper Cocktail

Hop Frog Cocktail

Hop Toad Cocktail

Horse's Neck Cocktail

Jackrabbit Cocktail

Kicking Cow Cocktail / *pg. 99*

Kitty Cocktail

Lamb's Wool Cocktail

Leap Frog Cocktail

Lizard Skin Cocktail

Monkey Gland Cocktail / *pg. 120*

Mule Cocktail

Mule's Hind Leg Cocktail

Panther's Breath Cocktail / *pg. 130*

Peacock Cocktail

Prairie Chicken Cocktail / *pg. 149*

Serpent's Tooth Cocktail

Shark's Tooth Punch

Swan Cocktail

Tiger's Milk Cocktail

White Elephant Cocktail

White Lion Cocktail

Yellow Parrot Cocktail

Yellow Rattler Cocktail

ZOMBIE
Punch

❄ TO QUASH AN OVERLY WILD FÊTE ❄

Any time a party gets out of hand and a police visit is nigh, whip up a batch of this: Zombie Punch is a surefire guarantee that your fête will make the turn from *Animal House* to *Night of the Living Dead* in no time.

The recipe—adapted from one found in Trader Vic's 1947 *Bartender's Guide*—will subdue approximately sixty people:

TWO 750-ML BOTTLES JAMAICAN RUM

FOUR 750-ML BOTTLES PUERTO RICAN RUM

ONE 750-ML BOTTLE DEMERERA RUM

TWO 750-ML BOTTLES CURAÇAO

3 QUARTS FRESH LEMON JUICE

3 QUARTS FRESH ORANGE JUICE

1 QUART GRENADINE

2 OUNCES PERNOD

CAKE OF ICE

———

Mix ingredients thoroughly; chill with a large cake of ice in an oversized punch bowl. Let it stand an hour or two before serving. If party is still out of control, consider turning to any one of the Miltown cocktails detailed on page 141.

———

Serves at least 60

FURTHER READING

Several of these books are out of print, but can be easily scouted through secondhand book vendors or accessed in library archives. Some of the older titles below have been re-issued, but the date listed here indicates the earliest date of publication—usually the edition used to research this book.

ADAMS, JAD.
Hideous Absinthe: A History of the Devil in a Bottle.
New York: I.B. Taurus & Co., Ltd., 2004.

BEEBE, LUCIUS.
The Stork Club Bar Book.
New York: Rinehart & Co., 1946.

BROWN, JOHN HULL.
Early American Beverages.
New York: Bonanza Books, 1966.

CASE, CARLETON B.
The Big Toast-Book: A Compendium of the Best New and Old Toasts, Sentiments, Quotations and Merry Quips.
Chicago: Shrewesbury Publishing Co., 1927.

CRADDOCK, HARRY.
The Savoy Cocktail Book.
London: Constable & Company, 1930.

CROCKETT, ALBERT STEVENS.
The Old Waldorf-Astoria Bar Book, With Amendments Due to the Repeal of the XVIIIth.
New York: A.S. Crockett, 1935.

EDITORS OF *ESQUIRE* MAGAZINE.
Esquire's Handbook for Hosts.
New York: Grosset & Dunlap, 1949.

FIELD, COLIN PETER.
The Cocktails of the Ritz Paris.
New York: Simon & Schuster, 2003.

FLEXNER, MARION W.
Cocktail-Supper Cookbook.
New York: M. Barrows and Company, Inc., 1955.

HIRSCHFELD, AL.
The Speakeasies of 1932 (Original title: *Manhattan Oases*).
New York: E.P. Dutton & Co., Inc., 1932.

TERRINGTON, WILLIAM.
Cooling Cups and Dainty Drinks.
New York: George Routledge and Sons, 1869.

THOMAS, JERRY.
The Bon Vivant's Companion . . . Or . . . How to Mix Drinks.
New York: Dick and Fitzgerald, 1862.

TRADER VIC.
Bartender's Guide By Trader Vic.
New York: Doubleday & Company, Inc., 1947.

ACKNOWLEDGMENTS

I wish to express my appreciation to the fellow imbibers who contributed their thoughts, suggestions, recipes, and well-wishes: Emily Haynes, Kate Lee, Gregory Macek, Luke Ives Pontifell, Slater Gillin, Glynnis MacNicol, Jesse Sheidlower, Thom Collins, Sarah Rosenberg, Jennifer Lynn Pelka, Cator Sparks and Emily Arden Wells.

Heartfelt thanks as well to the New York Public Library; the St. Regis New York; Thornwillow Press, Ltd.; Eleven Madison Park; Left Bank Books; Gastronomista; Bonnie Slotnik Cookbooks; and Joanne Hendricks Cookbooks, whose resources and troves of literature about historical libations greatly informed this work.

ABOUT LESLEY M. M. BLUME

Lesley M. M. Blume is an author, journalist, and cultural observer based in New York City. Her first edition of *Let's Bring Back*—an encyclopedia celebrating hundreds of forgotten-yet-delightful objects, fashions, culinary delectables, and personalities—debuted to critical acclaim in 2010 ("Whimsical . . . comical . . . delightful." – *The New Yorker*).

She adores a Gin Fizz in the summer, a Hot Toddy in the winter, and a fine glass of Champagne at any time of the year.

Learn more about her at *www.lesleymmblume.com*.

INDEX

LIQUID MEASUREMENTS

DASH ·········· 6 DROPS

1 TSP (BAR SPOON) ········· $\frac{1}{6}$ OZ

1 TBSP (3 TSP) ············· $\frac{1}{2}$ OZ

2 TBSP (PONY) ··········· 1 OZ

3 TBSP (JIGGER) ··········· $1\frac{1}{2}$ OZ

$\frac{1}{4}$ CUP (4 TBSP) ············· 2 OZ ················· 60 ML

$\frac{1}{3}$ CUP (5 TBSP) ············· 3 OZ ················· 75 ML

$\frac{1}{2}$ CUP ················· 4 OZ ················· 120 ML

$\frac{2}{3}$ CUP ················· 5 OZ ················· 165 ML

$\frac{3}{4}$ CUP ················· 6 OZ ················· 180 ML

1 CUP ················· 8 OZ ················· 240 ML

1 PT (2 CUPS) ············· 16 OZ ············· 480 ML

1 QT (4 CUPS) ············· 32 OZ ············· 960 ML

750 ML BOTTLE ············· 25.4 OZ

1 LITER BOTTLE ············· 33.8 OZ

1 MEDIUM LEMON ··········· 3 TBSP JUICE

1 MEDIUM LIME ············· 2 TBSP JUICE

1 MEDIUM ORANGE ········· $\frac{1}{3}$ CUP JUICE